JOURNALISM AND GOVERNMENT

JOURNALISM
AND
GOVERNMENT

John Whale

Macmillan

First published 1972 by
THE MACMILLAN PRESS LTD
London and Basingstoke
Associated companies in New York Toronto
Dublin Melbourne Johannesburg and Madras

SBN 333 13315 3

Printed in Great Britain by
R & R CLARK LTD
Edinburgh

To J. L. W.

ACKNOWLEDGMENT

I am grateful to Harold Evans, the Editor of the *Sunday Times*, for allowing me time to write this book in the intervals of my work for the paper.

London, December 1971

CONTENTS

CHAPTER 1

A Field for Study

Ignorant, inaccurate, partisan even in presenting fact, negligent of the serious, tenacious of the trivial, greedy of bad news – journalists are worth studying, because study might remedy a few of their weaknesses; and that would be a result worth reaching, because their work can be important to the way the world is run.

No journalist of any length of service could deny that he has at one time or another earned all those labels. The question is how to achieve an improvement. You could establish a body with power to compel improvement. But wherever its power came from, its standards could not suit everyone: some people would still find that journalists were being allowed to put the wrong things in or leave them out; and since all power comes from the state in the end, the standards which would win would come from the state too, or from the people in charge of it at the time. Willingly or unwillingly, journalists would then grow ignorant of the state's failures, inaccurate about the size of its successes, partisan about its proposals, unamused even by the trivial unless it carried the state seal, and silent about bad news. There are countries where that happens already.

Reaching that point in the argument, journalists tend to suppose that there is no more to be said. Life in the confident Northcliffe tradition can go on.

But an encouraging movement in late years has been the growth, in the United States and now in Britain, of the study of broadcasting and newspapers by dons. University people, students as well as teachers, can examine the business of journalism without any of the risks which would flow from their having authority to put it right. Academics have no authority, after all, beyond the quality of their findings. But if their findings are clear enough, and their case against journalists sound enough, then a strong moral impulse is set up towards the only kind of reform likely to last or work: reform put in hand by journalists themselves.

What a working journalist can add to this study is a little experience of how journalists work, how they work on politicians, and how at least some of them see their function. Since my work has been with radio and television news programmes and a 'quality' newspaper, and mainly with the kind of news which makes up the subject-matter of politics, I think of those parts and topics of the trade in particular when I use the terms journalism and journalist.

The reason why journalism is worth saving from its sins is that it forms a first line of defence for the rule of reason in public affairs. That rule is now under insistent threat.

CHAPTER 2

The Defence of the Word

The decline of reason as a means of regulating affairs of state was neatly instanced by the struggle for Northern Ireland which began in earnest in February 1971. The Provisionals, or activists, of the Irish Republican Army had a reasonable case. So did the United Kingdom authorities. In the course of the year they both seemed to forget what their case was.

When the Provisionals began shooting British soldiers and setting off explosions which caused random death and injury in the streets and buildings of Belfast, they were maintaining a presence: they were asserting their title to be thought the defenders of Belfast's Catholic poor, as against the Official IRA or the Dublin Government or anybody else. If they remembered their aim of an all-Ireland socialist republic, they did not stop to ask themselves whether the ideals which made them want it were also served by the natural consequences of their actions. Was material advance their ideal? Then they were unwise to bring upon the community they sought to protect a slow run-down of those material solaces which it is the basic business of politics to provide: city transport, medical care, jobs, houses. Was the goal mental satisfaction? Then it was perverse that a lifetime's familiarity with violence and fear should be implanted in a new generation of the community's children.

The United Kingdom authorities were upholding the sanctity of law: an agreed frontier, a regional government elected by a large majority on the proposition that an all-Ireland state of any kind was to be avoided. The two main methods they chose were, first, the internment of suspected Provisionals or their sympathisers – without trial, without time limit, without publication of names, without statement of allegations, without systematic review of cases; and second, the questioning of suspects (many of whom were later let out as harmless) by means not so far known in the United Kingdom – making suspects lean against a wall by their fingertips for long periods, hooding them, subjecting them to continuous and monotonous noise, and depriving them of sleep and food.

Now during this time, besides flouting their own aims in this way, both sides showed a rising dislike of the journalists covering the combat. The Provisionals blew up newspaper offices, held up newspaper vans, and harassed individual reporters and cameramen. The United Kingdom authorities put it busily about that for journalists even to report facts, let alone to offer opinions, which reflected on the official line was plainly treasonous. A senior cabinet minister, meeting the editor of a major newspaper which had done both, greeted him – less than half in jest – as 'the Editor of the *IRA Gazette*'.

(There was a marked parallel here with the attitude of the United States authorities in the late sixties to public debate about administration policy in Vietnam. The country was at war: there could be no discussion of whether it ought to be fighting the war until the war was won. And if it was never won? Senior officers brought themselves to believe that a chief reason why it was never won was that journalists were allowed even to raise that doubt.)

It is understandable that combatants should be too busy to think. But it is a pity that they should try and prevent journalists from thinking, since journalists are the only people left on the scene who can do that job. No other voice can make itself heard quickly or loudly enough. The notion that there is any part to be played in the affair by reason must be first put forward in newspapers or on the air if at all.

In this instance, some journalists and news organisations took their opportunity, and some did not. After the first arrests of suspects for internment, it was the press which reported charges by some of them that they were cruelly treated; and a small committee of enquiry was set up under Sir Edmund Compton, a long-service public official. It was a newspaper which later reported even more serious charges, to the effect that the United Kingdom forces of order were using methods of 'psychological disorientation' on their prisoners: the Compton committee had discovered these already, but it is conceivable that British security men would have been able to expunge all mention of them from Sir Edmund's report if they had

IRISH TIMES

Reference to   P.S.

not already been made public. (Some other details were taken out.)

Besides this, there was a good deal of reporting which insisted on seeing as many sides of the question as could be seen: the reporters of *The Times*, the *Guardian* and the *Irish Times* of Dublin came particularly well out of the long struggle. Some newspaper opinion columns offered solutions worth examining and voiced appropriate warnings. A leader in the *Sunday Times* at the beginning of August, eight days before the internment arrests, said: 'Internment would worsen the army's chief problem, which is mass Catholic hostility. Most important, it would carry the security forces beyond the frontier of what is ordinarily considered tolerable in a civilised society.' It did both. The effect on hopes for reconciling the Catholic community to the existing order was disastrous.

On the other hand, there were newspapers which would have felt quite at home among the jingo press as it existed in Britain during the Boer War or at the outset of the First World War. Our boys were magnificent, their opponents were devils, and that was that: there could be no possible consideration of whether the cause for which either side fought was well based. These newspapers found nothing but comfort in the Compton committee's remarkable use of words about the interrogation techniques. Yes, there was ill-treatment, the committee concluded, but not brutality: brutality is in the mind. 'We consider that brutality is an inhuman or savage form of cruelty, and that cruelty implies a disposition to inflict suffering, coupled with indifference to, or pleasure in, the victim's pain. We do not think that happened here.'

Certain broadcasting units resigned themselves to another departure from reason. They submitted to a form of self-censorship. The BBC's top men in particular seemed to have forgotten how, during the Second World War, the Corporation had taught the Government to tell something like the truth and profit by it: bad figures for aircraft losses early in the war made good figures believable later. Now a whole system of rules and checks within the Corporation made it in practice very hard for BBC reporters to talk to Provisional sympathisers. For a notional gain in military morale, the authorities lost a precious insight into thought and feeling on the other side.

*

Pleading in *Areopagitica* for uncensored discussion of public affairs, John Milton described the written word which carried it as 'the breath of reason itself'. He was thinking chiefly of the books and pamphlets which then carried much of the public debate. But he did not exclude (although he did not admire) the news books or mercuries which in 1644 were already beginning to appear as the forerunners of weekly journalism; and his phrase took on a new aptness three hundred years later, when broadcast journalism added spoken to written discussion. It was already a laden image, because it implied that reason in this sense was not indestructible: it had an existence which was no less fragile than a human life.

Like many people since, Milton did not find the issue of censorship a simple one. He was arguing – unsuccessfully, as it turned out – against the Long Parliament's demand that written work should be licensed before it was published. But he seems to have seen no bar to prosecution afterwards – notably of 'that which is impious or evil absolutely either against faith or manners', in which he included popery. And it is true that censorship, before or after publication, is not for the writer or broadcaster the ultimate deprivation. The censor's pencil is at any rate a recognition that the written or the spoken word can influence thought and action. The word is powerful: therefore it must be struck through.

There is a far more debilitating and dangerous attack that can be made against the word as a means of arranging public affairs. This attack, which may prove to be one of the distinguishing marks of the second half of the twentieth century, has also become known as a retreat: the retreat from the word. Sympathisers with this movement claim that the word is not so much censorable as contemptible: it has seldom achieved political change by itself, and has now lost what general usefulness it ever had. The word is powerless: therefore it must be neglected – in favour of more direct methods.

Arguments which support that conclusion have undoubtedly been piling up since the beginning of this century. As human motive became better understood, reasoning began to look vulnerable to self-interest and bias. Scholars perceived that even academic enquiry could not be wholly dispassionate: presuppositions were to some extent the product of circumstances.

The advancement of knowledge itself slowly ceased to seem the pure good which it had always been supposed. Nuclear physics made the atomic bomb: medicine, by keeping more people alive, made the population bomb. And since effective verbal reasoning was a pursuit which needed education, and few people had much of that, reasoning was seen by certain radicals as conspiratorial and tending to maintain the interests of the governing classes.

Some of the same charges could be laid against the vehicle of reason, language itself. For its highest effectiveness it depended on the shared literacy of a homogeneous class, who would understand not merely all the words but all the references contained in the words. When mass literacy inevitably brought a good deal of sub-literacy along with it, this quality was lost. Language has suffered other disabilities too. It has become specialised, to the point where certain specialists can only talk to other specialists working in the same corner of the same field. It has become insufficiently precise: many specialities in the sciences and even in philosophy are more and more pursued in symbols.

Trade and war have hastened this decline in precision. Language has been furred by advertising: words like 'luscious' or 'rugged' have lost part of their meaning, part of the distinct impression they once conveyed to the senses, for good. (One of the serious arguments in defence of the Welsh language, as against the English, is that as a language not worth advertising in – because the people who speak it and nothing else are few and poor – it has escaped the same impoverishment.) The usages of war degrade language further. When words can be used to make appalling realities less real – defoliation, deterrent capability, chemical and biological warfare (or even CBW) – then all words seem less trustworthy. Even Sir Edmund Compton, with his insistence that the inquisition methods he reported were not brutal enough to be called brutal, was adding his shovelful to the burial-mound of the word.

It will have been this kind of observation which impelled W. H. Auden to write recently, for a musical setting by Pablo Casals:

> Let mortals beware
> Of words, for
> With words we lie . . .

The lines were sung in New York in October 1971 to the United Nations – of all bodies the one which most needs a lively faith in the usefulness and trustworthiness of words. Yet the verse was a recognition of fact. A great many people concerned in public affairs have lost that faith, if they ever had it. And they are prepared to turn to other instruments for the furtherance of their aims.

The most common of these instruments, though not the only one, is violence or the threat of it: blowing up buildings, hijacking planes, kidnapping diplomats; and on the other side – since violence is as often deployed on behalf of the civil power as against it – the armed search, the snatch squad, the tank.

This is not new, in Ireland or anywhere else. It is a fair bet that the violence of any year in the 1970s could be paralleled from among the events of even the most seemingly peaceful year in the documented past. Europe before the lights went out for the First World War, for example, is widely regarded – even by people with a personal recollection of it – as living its last, long, golden afternoon. It was in fact in at least as disturbed a state as it is now. Testing this for a newspaper article in January 1971 I went, purely for mathematical neatness, to the files of *The Times* for January 1911. I lit on the police siege and killing of reputed anarchists at Sidney Street in the East End of London, an attempt to shoot the Prime Minister from the gallery of the French National Assembly, a student strike in Poland, and riotous strikes by Welsh miners and French champagne workers; to say nothing of bloodier riots in Mauritius, Bombay and Hankow, small wars in Peru and Morocco, and a demand by the New York coroner for severe gun control. The historians commissioned in 1968 to look into the origins of violence in America for the Eisenhower Commission on that theme found it necessary to go back to the Peasants' Revolt in England in 1381. No example of man's inhumanity to man, or of the fierce reaction to it, is wholly without precedent.

Two things that are new, though, are the destructiveness of modern weapons, even aside from nuclear weapons, and the fragility of modern developed life. There were sectarian riots in Belfast throughout the nineteenth century: what was new in the riots which brought in the British army in August 1969 was the Browning machine-gun. Again, air travel, piped water, electricity supply, are as easy to upset as they have become indispensable. That is the urban guerrilla fighter's opportunity. These things make it all the more vital for modern communities to replace violence with reason as a means of settling disputes.

The politics of reason has non-violent rivals too. The politics of manipulation is not confined to totalitarian countries. Even where the forms of democracy are scrupulously and peacefully maintained, attempts can be made to win votes by persuasions which have nothing to do with reason. To some extent this happens in all free elections: voters are frightened, charmed, cajoled. But the people who have literally made a business of it are political consultants in the United States. They exist because it is in effect possible to buy unlimited television time for political advertisement, because the cost of electioneering is thus inordinately high, and because candidates are therefore anxious to get the best value they can for their money by getting the best advice. Imitation will introduce the species into Europe even if similar conditions do not. The consultants claim to have discovered the philosopher's stone of politics: let them discover what kind of candidate the electorate wants and then arrange their man's campaign messages and car stickers accordingly, and they will transmute the base metal of a candidate – any candidate – into the pure gold of an elected representative of the people. Like the philosopher's stone, the idea originates in superstition and magic, and its record of demonstrable success is patchy. But it is a force for unreason, because it inclines politicians to resign their responsibility for reasoned argument at just the moment when it is most laid on them. If their consultant tells them that the way to win is to perambulate the state saying 'Vote for my opponent and keep crime rates high', they are likely to do it.

The International Association of Political Consultants, top-heavy with Americans, met in a London hotel in December 1970 to chew over their successes in the 1970 mid-term elections and gloss over their ill-successes. The most noticeable body of Europeans there were the French, who were in a position to maintain that French elections were fought with all the psychological subtlety you could want – had not Jacques Chaban-Delmas, the Prime Minister, used claret-coloured posters in his recent by-election victory in Bordeaux? – but with all the proper incitements to thoughtfulness in the electorate as well. Something of a divide opened between the old world and the new. As the conference broke up, the French first-string said to the ablest of the younger Americans:

'You are a clever boy, Mike, but you 'ave to read Pascal and Descartes.'

'I already did Pascal and Descartes,' the American said. 'I'm on Bucky Fuller and McLuhan.'

The exchange may have presented European politics in too intellectual and American politics in too unintellectual a light; but the champions were accurately chosen – the two seventeenth-century Frenchmen, exploring the potentialities of reason, over against two twentieth-century North Americans, proclaiming the beneficence of technology.

The high proportion of nonsense in McLuhan, at any rate, is now much more generally recognised than it was; and political consultants who follow him need not in themselves be seen as outriders of a new invasion of unreason. The danger, such as it is, of their nostrums taking effect is largely removed as soon as all political candidates employ them. The moment both battle-lines are equipped with witch-doctors of similar qualifications, the battle can be resumed on the old terms. Yet even if the struggle is not distorted, it can still be debased. If both parties in a campaign seek to persuade the voter to choose their man because he gives off a general aura of strength and kindliness, rather than because his actions and words suggest some reasonable expectation that he will think sensible thoughts in office and do sensible things, then the whole level of debate is lowered: beguilement is substituted for argument.

These methods are not new, either. Half-truths have been told on behalf of rulers or aspirant rulers since Alexander the Great. (Such techniques are more often used to sustain the existing order than to overthrow it: revolutionaries can seldom pay the fees.) But they cheapen the word; they give life to a view of public affairs which public men ought not to hold; and they are spreading.

In great things and small, then, the movement against reason is a fact, even if not a totally new fact; and the journalist's business is to resist it. There are other people who can discharge the task with more authority in the end – politicians, public servants, specialist academics, historians; but the task falls to the journalist sooner than to them, because of the frequency of publication, and less avoidably. He is not ill equipped for the exercise: words are his chosen weapons. He ought to confront the partisans of violence, official or insurgent, with the deeds done in their name and the alternatives still open. He ought to see that the whole facts of a politician's case are presented. He ought to be a steward of the word.

CHAPTER 3

Irrelevant Miracles

Journalists hang together. Radio and television people are avid readers of newspapers: newspaper reporters take down broadcast words. Raw material and methods are very much the same: both groups ask the same kind of questions. The essential instrument is the same: the word. Broadcasting is at least as dependent on it as newspapers are. A radio report may make effective use of the sound of church bells; but until the commentary explains that they are rung by citizens welcoming the liberating forces, the sound goes for nothing. Television news searches all the time for pictures; but where they are not simply pictures of men uttering words, they are likely to lean heavily, for their effect, on the words underneath. Show the same seascape on two separate occasions. Say the first time that these waters are to be desalted for tap-water, and the second time that they have ruined local fishermen because they are too dirty to support fish. To the eye, linked as it is to the brain, the two pictures will look different.

Yet there is a difficulty about television. It is fairly clear that radio has enough affinity with newspapers to make it worthwhile to consider them together: much of what is said on the air in news and current affairs programmes is written down first, and BBC radio at any rate still keeps enough of its literate past about it to be able to fill the greater part of a weekly newspaper – the *Listener* – with broadcast words. There is less certainty that television is on all fours with newspapers in the same way, or can sensibly be studied along with the other two for the way it works in public affairs. Its reach, and its likely effect, seem so very much larger than theirs. Is not the whole nature of political communication being steadily changed by television and its attendant electronic gadgetry?

This is the intelligible ten per cent of McLuhanism, made familiar in that reverberating phrase about the global village.

The notion is that television puts us all in constant touch: one country with another, the ruler with the ruled; and instantaneously. That must have its effect on international and domestic politics, to look no further.

So it might, if the premise about the larger reach were true. Television might become an immensely powerful advocate of rational discussion and decision, able to make sure that pretty well everyone commanded the necessary evidence; or it might become – would become, if the rest of the McLuhan edifice about audio-tactile stimuli and so on stood up – a crushing contribution to the politics of unreason. A tyrant would only need to tickle our audio-tactile stimuli and we would roll over on our backs.

But the premise is false; so the whole question of what the effect might be falls to the ground. Not merely is the notion of the all-pervasiveness of television not true; it is becoming less true all the time.

The last story I ever covered as a television news reporter also happened to be the last occasion (it is reasonable to hope) when United Kingdom troops invaded another country. The date was March 1969. The place was Anguilla, a flat and ugly island in the West Indies: in a rush of blood to the head Labour's then Foreign Secretary, Michael Stewart, was anxious to cleanse it of bad men. From a narrow professional point of view the invasion was a delight. There was no difficulty about getting on to the island ahead of the troops: the dawn landing was made where local opinion thought it would be, and when there was already enough light to film by: plenty of guns were to be seen, but not one of them was fired: the seizure of the airport did not stop small charter planes from flying peacably in and out to take the film away. Despite this untypical good luck, despite absorbed British interest, despite its all happening in an area of heavy international travel, film of the invasion was only scrambled on to British television screens twelve hours later. At that, it had made a perfect journey, with a tight connection in San Juan and fast processing in New York before being beamed up to the trans-Atlantic satellite.

The notable point was that it had to go to New York at all. If the global-village view were true, the job could have been done from Anguilla itself, or at the least from one of the other

Leeward Islands. But it needed a television station with developing and editing equipment, a land link to the satellite, and technicians who knew what to do. The Leeward Islands are not so blest. The nearest such station was two thousand miles away in New York. And even when the pictures reached London, they could not expect to be shown for longer than the remaining few minutes of the evening news bulletin (*News at Ten*), because advertisements and the next programme were waiting to come on. A television set is not a device for plucking whatever you like out of the air whenever you like, and it will not become one. The technical and economic limits are too strict. The events which can be dipped into as they happen are predictable and often banal: the inauguration of a President, the investiture of a Prince of Wales.

Television expands, true. A global satellite system has been in place since the summer of 1969: a satellite now hangs above each of the three great oceans of the world – Atlantic, Indian and Pacific – and can therefore be reached from any point on the globe where there is access to a ground station. More and more countries have such stations: they are useful for telephone as well as television traffic. Over forty countries were expected to have them by the end of 1972. Another stage is distributional satellites, which will deliver the same programme simultaneously to several different television stations in the same country or continent – the job now done for television networks by land-lines and microwave relays. The Russians already have a system of this kind. After that may come satellites which can broadcast direct to television sets: 1985 is the date when the trade expects the trick to be technically and economically workable.

The arguments which have swirled round this range of talking stars rise in great part out of commercial fears: cable and wireless companies are afraid of losing business to satellites, European countries are afraid of American dominance in the international satellite consortium. But the idea of a space satellite which can send signals straight to the aerial on the bungalow roof has roused fears of a different kind. If the signals start in the same country as they end, there is no more problem about regulating them than there is about more usual kinds. But the signals can just as easily start in some other country. Then the fear would be of deliberately hostile broadcasting: perversion by cultural radicalism, or subversion by incitement to discontent.

To judge from the record, there is not much cause for alarm. France is probably the most broadcast-into country in the world; and the radio and television broadcasters who pour their wares into the hexagon of French mainland territory from Luxembourg, and the Saar, and Monaco, and Andorra, have been doing it simply to beat French rules against commercial broadcasting, and have stayed as far from cultural radicalism as they can.

The world's experience with hostile or strategic radio broadcasting is no more of a kind to make existing régimes tremble. Whatever else turned the Germans out of France at the end of the Second World War, it was not the broadcasts made to the French people from London. General de Gaulle's first broadcast in June 1940 became important afterwards in the theology of Gaullism as the occasion when he declared himself the legitimate national leader; but very few people seem to have heard it at the time. Not long after he returned to power in May 1958 he closed down the corresponding service in Paris, the Section Anglaise of the French national radio; and to me at least, as a very junior member of its staff near the end, his judgment seemed sound. Most of the known audience were radio hams, interested that they could pick up the short-wave signals a great way off and totally uninterested by the news we relayed to them from French Ministry of Information material. (It could hardly be called raw material, and yet it could not fairly be described as cooked either. It was selected.) The new President chose to pursue his old struggle with the Anglo-Saxons by more direct methods: excluding Britain from the Market, evicting NATO from France.

Other governments seem to have come to the same kind of conclusion. The two American radio stations which (apparently with Central Intelligence Agency support) began lobbing their messages over the Iron Curtain from Munich in the early fifties – Radio Liberty to Russia and Radio Free Europe to Soviet satellite countries – soon abandoned their hope of fostering revolt. They were partly sobered by the fate of the Hungarian rising in 1956. And the British Government's attempt to broadcast from Botswana into recalcitrant Rhodesia during 1966 ended after a few months in quiet failure.

If television ever had any greater chance than radio of becoming the doomsday weapon of psychological warfare, the chance is already fast being lost. When television began, its spread as a social habit was dazzling. Whole nations knew about the same programmes. Between 1947 and 1955 the number of television licences in the United Kingdom went up from 14,000 to nearly five million, and the country still had only one television channel. French television in the fifties had one programme on its sole channel which left all the others behind in popularity: a monthly current affairs show called *Cinq Colonnes à la Une*. Its title implied that the news stories it examined would rate five columns on the front page of any newspaper. It went out on a Friday. Box-office takings in Paris theatres fell so heavily on the first Friday of each month that theatre managers pleaded for the programme to be shifted to a Tuesday, the night when most of the theatres closed.

Those days are gone. Not merely has the newness and the shared excitement vanished, but television can never again as a matter of course deliver a national audience; and this has meaning for domestic as well as international politics. It kills the idea of the television referendum, or the mesmeric television demagogue, as surely as it kills the idea of foreign aggression by direct broadcast. What has happened to the audience is that it has been fragmented. In 1964 the number of television channels in Britain increased to three, and in France to two, besides the commercial stations just outside France's borders. In most American cities you can get three stations which deliver the national networks, and a handful of local stations besides. There are occasions when most of these channels are showing the same thing: throughout the world the first American moon landing, in July 1969, was the clearest example; but in the ordinary way to gather even a third of the potential audience for a current affairs programme is a considerable feat.

As the number of television channels increases, under the inevitable pressure from people who want to work or make money in television, the audience will be further divided; and the process will become faster as each television set becomes able to accommodate more sources of pictures – home video recording, which enables you to see an old programme again; cassettes, which you can get from a shop or a library; cable, which brings you from a nearby collecting point a much greater variety of material than you can get over the air, including information drawn from data banks run by computers. Instead of all watching the same transmission, as they did in the beginnings of television, people will then be watching innumerable different transmissions at once. So far from gathering the audience, electronic circuitry will disperse it.

For the moment, though, the job of splitting up the television audience is safely in the hands of television's own urge for more and more channels. Those other devices are very expensive. Applying inventions costs huge sums of money, and the money has to come out of private even more than public purses. The first telephone exchange in Britain was opened in 1879, and telephone wire is much cheaper than the coaxial cable which cable television needs; yet more than ninety years later there were still telephones in only a third of British homes.

That is part of the difficulty, too, about the common supposition that television can solve the world's problems through education. Exactly the peoples of the world who might be thought to need this service most are the ones who can afford it least. They need more than television sets, in any case. The experience of the Open University in Britain has shown that a television set can provide a student with a focus, with guidance, perhaps even with fellowship; but he still needs books, in the same numbers as he would if he were at a more ordinary university.

There is a misty belief that electronics have made it possible for the sum of human knowledge to be gathered together in one place, like water in a great reservoir, and tapped off by television sets in the privacy of the igloo, the corrugated-iron shack or the semi-detached. But who decides what is knowledge, to be included in the data bank, and what is either mis-statement or sheer opinion? – because the man in that position becomes a very powerful man indeed. Or is every last published word poured into it, from the *Annual Register* to the *News of the World*? – a daunting print-out for anyone who presses the button. What language do the mysteries come out in? – since if the effect were only a new Anglo-Saxon cultural imperialism, it would create as many problems as it solved.

A data bank is no more than a public library on skates: a

fallible compilation of all kinds of recorded work, limited by the funds and the imagination and the learning of the people who compile it, and with its treasures accessible only by choice and effort. The push given to it by electronics is only added speed: the struggling messengers of the British Museum Reading Room are replaced by printed circuits.

Speed, in the end, is the only thing television can offer in the future beyond what it offers at present. Electronic cameras will more and more replace film cameras, so that pictures can be transmitted at once without needing to be developed. Satellites will more and more replace land-lines, so that pictures can be sent further in a single hop. Cassettes or cable might one day allow the historian to look back over the past without the bother of going to the library or the television company's archives. These are differences in degree, not in kind.

Fragments of television memoirs published in the seventies re-create the sense of delighted astonishment which television professionals felt in the fifties at the prowess of their new toy. They never asked themselves why they were down a coal-mine or up a light-house: it was enough that they could send instantaneous pictures. 'La folie du direct', one French television administrator called it. But the first raptures of revolution never come back.

Instantaneous broadcasting from remote places is a conquest of space. Recording, on magnetic tape, with pictures as well as sound, is a conquest of time: almost a conquest of death, in that we can still see the brothers Kennedy, or Nikita Khrushchev, or Charles de Gaulle, in their habits as they lived. Both these marvels date from the early fifties. Television's truly magical innovations are behind it.

CHAPTER 4

The Primacy of the Press

If it is true that television's range will not now increase significantly, then there is a case for saying that newspapers have survived the coming of broadcasting to remain the leading means of communication in public affairs. The case is only worth making at the outset because it indicates where the responsibilities of leadership rest.

If the race were to the swift, newspapers would not have a chance. Technical progress is a struggle they often seem to have given up. British newspapers do as well as those of any other Western country in improving, with computers and cameras, a technology which was invented in the fifteenth century and brought substantially to its present state in the nineteenth. But the flag of advance is flown in the provinces, not the capital: interested foreigners are taken to Hemel Hempstead, not Fleet Street; and the ideas which British national newspapers ought to have been looking at are in full use in Japan. The system of printing by remote control at a second location which is now used by Japan's leading daily paper, *Asahi Shimbun*, was in fact devised for the *Manchester Guardian* before it began to print in London in September 1960; but the *Guardian* did not use it.

People who make a business of peering into the future like to look forward to a time when newspapers are delivered to each subscribing household electronically. Successive sheets will fall from a televisual photocopier inside the front door. But the vision is slow in materialising; and meanwhile more ordinary methods of delivery continue unimproved. In many parts of continental Europe, as in rural Britain, the only way to get a newspaper delivered to your door is to have it brought by the postman – yesterday's paper at twice the price. In urban Britain and America your paper is delivered by child labour, if at all. In Britain the child is normally employed by a local newsagent, who can exercise some supervision; and the culture dictates that the paper should be dropped near the front door, if not through it. In America the child is employed by the newspaper itself, so that the supervision is more distant; and custom asks no more than that the paper should be thrown towards the door. In bad weather it can be unreadable when recovered.

Written news will never travel as fast as broadcast news. Its edge is not speed but penetration. Reading has this advantage in particular over listening, that it can be done in the reader's own time. To him an interruption or a distraction is merely a delay. But distraction is peculiarly damaging to the listener, because the moment of inattention cannot be made up.

The spoken word on television and radio runs a constant gauntlet of distractions. On television it has to compete not just with the pictures but with all the trivial alarums of domestic life. Radio lives on distractions, in the sense that what has saved it from extinction in the television age is the fact that you can do something else as well as listen to it – drive a car, bake a cake. Anyone who has listened to the news as he drives is aware that he has sometimes missed a detail because he has been attending to a child crossing the road, a traffic light, another car. Just as well, too.

It would be absurd to decry the power of the spoken word. One of the most powerful poems in the history of man, the *Iliad*, almost certainly began its life before the invention of writing. Its mere existence is proof that it triumphed over the natural inattentiveness of its after-dinner audiences in ill-lit Aegean banqueting-halls. But the rhapsode who declaimed a story from it had a number of advantages not vouchsafed even to television newscasters.

He was a rare presence, although his story had a delightful half-familiarity to his listeners. More than that, he was a real presence. He compelled attention where a moving photograph only asks for it. He would notice the discourtesy of inattentiveness. But also he was there. He supplied a verbal image of the battlefields beyond the firelight; but he was not himself an image. If he had been on a television set in the corner of the hall, his story would have been at a double remove from the real: images furnished by an image.

There is another Hellenic parallel for television, drawn a few hundred years later by Plato with chilling foreknowledge. In the *Republic*, he ascribes to Socrates a long simile designed to show the great distance which the natural man must travel before he attains a state of reasoned understanding. Shackled prisoners in a cave see pictures projected on a wall in front of them. The projector is a fire behind them: the objects are carried on the heads of people walking past it. The technology is of the cinema: the prisoners are in the front stalls, and the carriers (as far as the simile is clear) parade across the back of the circle, with only their burdens in line with the light from the projection-box. But the product is television. The objects, images of men and beasts and instruments, recur on a partially predictable pattern, and are taken by the prisoners to be real. In fact they are not just images but images of images; and the slow process of learning which Plato – never an admirer of the common man – proposes for his prisoners is that they should look first of all at the original or material images, then (their eyes dazzled by exposure to the daylight) at the shadows of real objects in the real world outside, then at the real objects themselves, and finally – only for choice spirits, this – at the sun, which represents the controlling source of goodness and intelligence. Then they are ready to go back down the rocky slope into the cave and start spreading the news – with the likelihood of getting killed for their pains. (Plato allows Socrates, his narrator in the dialogue, that much foreknowledge of a more immediate future. By the time the *Republic* was written, Socrates had already been executed for the insistent radicalism of his teaching.)

Images of images? True of a television play, clearly. Not always true of television news. The film camera often shows things which would have been there anyway as part of the real world. But people are very seldom quite unconscious of anything as obtrusive as a sixteen-millimetre sound film camera, and much that is shown on news bulletins is a modification of normality with television in mind: an interview, a press conference, a street protest, a pause in a doorway. A television interview or discussion, the standard tool of investigation and reporting, is a representation on the screen of a representation in front of cameras of how two or three people might have talked if they had been by themselves. It is not in any important sense fraudulent, since the viewers understand all this if they bother to formulate it: they are better off than the shackled prisoners in the darkened cave; but it is an image of an image.

The printed word, on the other hand, is not an image. It is as direct a representation of thought as speech is, and more controllable. Further, its subject matter is not an image, or need not be. Out of sloth or necessity, writing journalists sometimes use an arranged situation like a press conference; but they can live without it, and their work is better if they do.

The philosophical arguments for the primacy of the printed word thus shade into the practical. Making the change from television to newspaper work, I have been struck by how much less easy it is for a television reporter to find out what has happened or is happening than it is for a newspaper reporter.

It is not simply that I can get about better now: that I am one instead of at least three, that I have no camera crew with me whose movements I delay and who delay mine, that the luggage with me need consist only of a suitcase and a typewriter instead of more than a dozen bulky boxes. It is not even that getting a story into a newspaper is so much less arduous a business than getting a piece of television on to the air: a typewriter and a telephone replace the whole rigmarole of aeroplane and satellite and film labs and viewing theatres and editing machines, with the result that the reporter has much more time to work in before the material need leave his hand. What counts is the psychological difference between a camera, or any recording device, and a notebook. You notice it as soon as you sit down with someone who can tell you what you want to know. If there is a camera behind you, your man is aware that he is not really talking to you at all. He is talking to anyone who might be listening, total strangers, his family, his employers, his voters. His words are guarded, self-conscious. It is the same if there is a microphone in front of him, and two rotating rolls of magnetic tape slowly recording the sound for radio (or even for use in a newspaper; but if they are, then the newspaper has only itself to blame for their uninformativeness, since the published question-and-answer form belongs now to broadcasting if anywhere).

It is not the same if the only piece of recording equipment produced is a notebook. Even if he is self-conscious at first, your informant quickly sees that not everything he says is written down. (Not everything he says can be written down, since as a rule the only reporters whose shorthand can compass a verbatim transcript of any length have perfected it over long years in law court or parliamentary press gallery, and are in consequence imprisoned there still.) There will be gaps – there may be long gaps – between the interesting or important things he says; and in consequence there will be long periods while the notebook is unused, and he rapidly forgets so apparently innocuous a device in his admirable anxiety that you should see the affair in hand as he does.

There are many occasions when a newspaper reporter need not use a notebook at all until after the talk is over. Storing the mind with things said, like a chipmunk filling its cheeks with maize, and then disgorging them on to the pages of a notebook, is a technique comparatively easily learnt. It has the advantage that it makes not merely the answers flow more readily but the questions too, since the reporter is not half-preoccupied with writing down the answer to one question while he devises the next. It can only be used if the results of the interview are either not going to be quoted at all or quoted anonymously, since for attributed quotation it is not precise enough. But those are often the most interesting quotations – too revealing, or too damaging, to be fathered on their originator without his express permission: the borough architect's reflection on his council's collective taste, the backbencher's unease about the party leadership.

Television reporters hear that kind of observation at least as often as newspaper reporters – perhaps more often, in moments of post-interview relaxation, when the subject is relieved and a little surprised at having guarded himself so well from indiscretion. But television reporters cannot use it. They have to use the interview itself instead, the discreet bromide. Those are the terms on which they got it.

That ought to mean, none the less, that television reporters are at least as well informed as newspaper reporters about the detail of the scene they cover. But it does not: they are spared having to write it in detail. Writing about something, as a means to learning it, beats even teaching: areas of vagueness are less easy to dissimulate. As a television reporter, I very seldom needed to know about anything in detail, because I very seldom wrote about anything in detail. When four hundred words – less than the length of this printed page – is a long piece, detail is dispensable.

The cant in the trade, not wholly discouraged by broadcast journalists, is that it is more difficult and time-consuming to write briefly than to write at length. So it might be, if the same volume of information and ideas had to be packed into the short piece as into the long one. But there is no question of that in broadcasting. It was natural for a crime reporter on a popular paper to get as many facts as he could into his piece about an obscure MP who was acquitted in May 1970 on a spying charge: 'The former pit boy, who had admitted receiving £2,300 from the Czechs in eight years, walked from the dock after the 13-day trial. Twenty minutes later he was smuggled out of a side entrance on his way home to a ham-salad tea at his semi-detached house in Woodstock Road, Carshalton.' Even the worst of broadcasters would discover that a spoken offering could not be quite so full of currants and stay digestible. And since he did not need to use so many facts, he would not need to discover them either. He would have the extra time to get his stuff back to the office instead.

If that scrap of testimony is accepted, it contains the germ of an answer to the claim that most people in developed countries get the bulk of their information about public affairs from television. The bulk of the information is not on television. If people do indeed understand and retain what they learn from television, then their understanding will be in broad terms at best.

The rest of the answer is partly flippant. It is that television gets most of its news ideas from newspapers anyway, so people who get their news from television are in fact getting it from newspapers at one remove. In so far as this is true, it is to some extent unavoidable. News bulletins come round more often than once a day: many broadcast journalists have less time to find things out in than newspapermen have, technical pressures aside. For just the same reasons, daily newspapermen draw on the information in weekly papers. Further, there is the simple point that broadcasters find it a great deal easier to consult newspaper archives than their own. Newspaper cuttings have a convenient physical existence, and television news organisations have cuttings libraries hard by their newsrooms. Re-running an old news bulletin, or even the tape-recording usually taken of it, is a much more arduous business. That is part of the pre-eminence of the printed word. Anthropologists date the dawn of civilisation from the moment when the spoken word could be written down. It could then be looked at again. The community's wisdom became cumulative, not evanescent.

Clearly, newspapermen draw on television too. Few newspapermen do anything on election nights except watch television. The results of televised sporting fixtures are regularly taken from the screen. It would be pointless labour to do anything else, when the evidence is already so well gathered. And television's capacity to harvest its own news can only increase. What has partly held back the development of the necessary specialist reporters has been the difficulty (given a news bulletin's small compass) of finding them enough to do, and hence of training them to do it with enough aplomb.

Another reason why television journalism retains few staff thinkers is that most thinking journalists like an occasional chance to say what they think, and the chances on television are few or none. Newspapermen have plenty of opportunities, if they want them: editorials, signed leader-page articles, diary or note-book entries, to say nothing of the kind of reporting of sport or the arts which is chiefly a critique of performance: anywhere where the reader is made aware that he is being offered a statement of opinion rather than of fact. (It can happen even within news reports, if the reporter feels that his own coming down on one side of the question or the other is itself an event worth noticing. When *The Times* abandoned anonymity, it was the paper's most senior correspondents who most freely larded their copy with the first-person pronoun.)

Television reporters are less lucky. The special genius of the form demands that their report should be chiefly drawn up in terms of the comparative objectivity of pictures. More than that, television news bulletins and current affairs programmes are not rich in opportunities for staff men to unload their opinions. There are no leading articles, no expressions of editorial view, on British television. The BBC and the independent television companies are specifically forbidden to voice their own views. The prohibition is in the Television Act and in the terms on which the BBC's licence is from time to time renewed.

And there would almost certainly be no editorials even if no such prohibition were in force. Commercial television in the United States is free of it, and uses the freedom sparingly. Broadcasters all over the world have too strong a sense of officialdom peering over their shoulder – the same officialdom which allows their organisation a licence to broadcast and a frequency to broadcast on, and whose benevolence is therefore worth retaining. Whether in an editorial or a piece of reporting, an opinion which is not balanced by a contrary opinion may call down sour looks from people in government. But to counterbalance the opinion of an editorialist, or even a staff reporter, in this way is to voice total self-mistrust. Better to leave the whole thing alone.

Newspapers are no strangers to official displeasure; but in most Western countries they can afford to be undismayed by it, because they are not dependent for their very existence on official goodwill. Certainly a ban on editorialising in newspapers would be thought as odd as it is thought unsurprising in broadcasting.

For a newspaper, the freedom to editorialise is extremely useful (quite aside for the moment from the question of whether it is effective). It allows a newspaper to react to an item of news, a politician's speech, a government proposal, more overtly than by merely putting it at the top of page one or the bottom of page five. The newspaper can make it clear that it prints the news with enthusiasm, with reservations, or with distaste. When Anthony Wedgwood Benn accused Enoch Powell, during the 1970 election, of hoisting in Wolverhampton – with his 'obscene racialist propaganda' – the same flag that fluttered over Dachau and Belsen, *The Times* carried what must have been one of the shortest leaders in its history. It read, in full: 'We publish on another page an attack made last night on Mr. Powell by Mr. Benn. Though *The Times* has always strongly opposed Mr. Powell on immigration, we believe that this attack cannot conceivably be supported on the evidence of anything that Mr. Powell has said. We have decided to publish this attack because we believe that the fact and character of the attack, including its astonishingly intemperate language, should be known accurately to the public.'

The device enables the staff of a newspaper to disclose what kind of people they are. Newspaper leaders are arrived at in different ways in different newspaper offices. In some they result from a meeting of an editorial 'cabinet' which is not wholly unlike a ministerial cabinet, though a little less solemn: there is an opening statement from the member most concerned, discussion, a consensus identified from the editorial chair, and a member detailed to put it into effect in words. In some they result more often from a straightforward brief to the leader-writer from the editor. In no case could they for long be wholly at variance with what most other journalists on the paper could stand: either the staff would gradually change, or the leaders would. A leading article therefore becomes an expression of the highest common factor of opinion among most of the people on the paper's staff; and it is thus a signal to the reader, more rapid and reliable than he could collect from scanning the way items have been selected and presented, about what kind of paper he is reading. It is more than that: it is an acknowledgment that a newspaper is a live entity, with a mind of its own.

CHAPTER 5

An Opposition Voice

Before a big press conference begins, television cameramen will sometimes stalk the chamber with a silent-film camera in their hands to take a few pictures of the gathered newshawks. The pictures may later help the film editor to turn the occasion into an event; or he may simply need them as a cut-away, a link between one view of the main speaker and another. Newspapermen will happily lend themselves to this innocent deception: for the cameraman's benefit they will gaze attentively at the empty platform, or write a few words in their notebooks. A little later, when the platform has filled up and the conference has begun, it will be television's turn to do them a service: the television men will try to get all the main questions in at the outset, to lessen editing problems afterwards; and newspapermen are thus enabled to save their interventions for the extra detail or clarification which they need.

There are flashes of petulance between the two groups, when television equipment becomes too obtrusive or newspaper questions too prolix; but in general, on the ground, there is no feeling of rivalry, no assertion of dominance on one side or the other. However different their methods, their functions coincide.

The orthodox view of the journalistic function was set out by Francis Williams in his book *The Right to Know*, published the year before his death. 'The press has traditionally three linked responsibilities: to collect and publish the news, to interpret and comment on it, to act as a guard dog of the public interest in areas of public concern where executive power may be arbitrarily used.' He had the right to be respectfully heard: he had been a national newspaper editor and then a senior government servant, in war-time and peace-time. But this traditional statement of what the press does, or indeed of what news organisations in general do, leaves one or two things out of account. It suggests a picture of the governed arrayed against the government, and of journalists as mainly useful to the governed – sallying out to forage for news from the other side, predicting the enemy's movements, warning of his encroachments.

Yet in fact one of the main modern usefulnesses of news organisations is within government, without any reference to the governed. The most industrious readers of newspapers now, and the clients whom many journalists have in mind when they write about public affairs, are people in the industry of government – ministers, MPs, civil servants, service chiefs; and those people open their papers each morning not so much to see whether the governed are restless on the other side of the wire as to see what is being done in other corners of the same industry – foreign governments, friendly or not; unfriendly powers, outside the state or in it; subordinate or regional or local governments; alternative governments, in the shape of more or less loyal oppositions. They read about the governed too – often with a good deal more interest and anxiety than the governed read about them. At any rate in most Western countries, news organisations are not an arm of government in the sense of being at the Government's orders; but they are an indispensable instrument of government.

On the face of it, governments have diplomats to tell them what other governments are up to. Indeed, this is one of the main justifications for the huge establishments which all rich countries keep in each other's capitals. Diplomats exist to discover at least as much as to represent. The 105 assorted Russian officials ejected or barred from Britain in the autumn of 1971 for spying had in fact only been carrying the traditions of the trade beyond decent limits. But diplomats abroad use the newspaper and broadcasting stations of the capital as a principal source. One must not say so, because that would pull the rug from under the whole nineteenth-century charade: they are supposed to get their information from dinner-table badinage with the foreign minister's wife. But they would be unwise if they did not study the work of local journalists, who almost certainly see more of local politicians than the diplomats do. And their colleagues at home – the desk men for those parts – know perfectly well that this is the practice, because they did it themselves during their own last spell of duty in the field.

The home-based official – in Whitehall, for example – suspects, and rightly, that British journalists in the country concerned are using the same basic source. He nevertheless finds that he has to read or watch their reports. He knows that his superiors may well have seen them rather than any diplomatic traffic, so that there is a sense in which the events in them are the only ones which have happened. He further suspects that, although his own man's official contacts may be better than a journalist's, a journalist has one or two other sources besides.

In this he may well be right. The great strength of journalists in this context is that they can talk freely and decently to oppositions. This is not always easy for diplomats even in countries where the notion of a loyal opposition is understood. If British diplomats in Washington methodically went after their own information about what the policies of the next president were likely to be, attaching themselves to the rival candidates for long enough to find out, they would have to be careful not to be charged with interfering in American domestic politics. British reporters, on the other hand, do it all the time. And in countries where any opposition is branded disloyal – probably more than half the countries in the world – diplomats cannot talk to its representatives without looking positively seditious. The chief point of contact which those members have with the whole machinery of power is through journalists – especially foreign journalists.

The same point applies at home. Civil servants need to know about oppositions. They need to know what they must prepare for. Indeed, in Whitehall they have sometimes surprised incoming governments by the thoroughness with which they have prepared plans totally at variance with the plans of their previous masters. (Housing finance seems to have been a notable example in the 1970 changeover.) Yet beyond the occasional Athenaeum lunch they cannot frequent the company of shadow ministers. Journalists, on the other hand, can and do; and officials then get the message from newspapers and broadcasts.

All this has been clearest in Northern Ireland, which is in the strict sense both a domestic and a foreign problem for Britain: domestic, because it is part of the United Kingdom; foreign, because the government next most closely concerned after Britain is the Irish Government in Dublin, with the consequent involvement of the Foreign and Commonwealth Office, which also supplies the British Government's resident representative in Belfast. Foreign or domestic, the Government's most persistent problem has been to understand the opposition and the nature of its claims. The Protestant majority party which has ruled Northern Ireland without a break since 1921 takes as its aim the maintenance of Northern Ireland's union with Britain (which is to say its separateness from the Catholic Republic to the south). The party's name, Unionist, is also its only policy. All its actions, until the late sixties, were explicable in terms of that one aim. In consequence no opposition could oppose it without appearing to oppose the very make-up of the state. The notion of a loyal opposition became hard to sustain. Indeed, MPs elected on the non-Unionist side had a long history of declining to do the things which loyal oppositions are expected to do: they refused to take their seats, refused to go through the parliamentary motions. And of course they were disloyal, to the extent that they were non-Protestants and were critical of the end to which union with Britain was the means: Protestant ascendancy, finding its chief expression in the unfair distribution of jobs and public housing.

If that was indeed the inevitable end of those means, and the means were sacred, then it made no practical difference whether the opposition was heard or unheard. But if the same means might have been administered to a fairer end, then there would have been value in listening. The difficulty was that the British Government could barely even talk to the opposition, because of the obstacle of disloyalty; so British ministers could not discover whether there was a case to answer aside from the disloyalty. Not understanding that Protestant constitutionalism was a means to keep Catholics down, they could not be expected to understand that Catholic anti-constitutionalism was a means to avoid being kept down.

It was a situation in which the opposition had no recourse except to news organisations. For a long time journalists took no great notice of them. (I can remember with some discomfort how, as late as the 1964 general election, I regarded Northern Ireland as the source simply of laughable electoral eccentricities, like nominating prisoners as candidates or 'polling the grave-yards' – marshalling the votes of people who were in fact dead.)

The first serious disorders, and the first serious newspaper notice of their causes, began to appear in the summer of 1966; but it was only in 1968 that the Catholic emancipation group who became the Northern Ireland Civil Rights Association compelled the attention of journalists by using the courageous device which Martin Luther King had first employed five years before in Alabama: the peaceful demonstration which could be relied on to provoke a non-peaceful response of a self-revelatory kind from the forces of order. And so it did, in Londonderry in October 1968 and at Burntollet in January 1969; and the news reports – whether or not out of a prurient interest in violence – showed a group of people with an unusually strong faith in the force of their grievances, and another group with an unusually strong interest in maintaining that those grievances were mere sedition; and the British Government saw to it that a Scottish judge, Lord Cameron, was set on to enquire into the basis of the grievance; and his finding that they were indeed well founded, that the Protestants had been fiddling electoral boundaries and council jobs and council houses for fifty years, was the text on which the British Government preached its first real reform sermon to the Northern Ireland Government in October 1969.

It all went wrong, of course. Even before the Cameron Commission reported, Protestant reaction against the new spiritedness among Catholics had become so fierce that it had brought British troops into Northern Ireland cities as peace-keepers and begun a vast increase in recruitment to the IRA Provisionals. By the spring of 1971 the troops and the Provisionals were engaged in a vicious war.

In this new situation journalists were even more central, or ought to have been. If it had been difficult for the British Government to discover what were the real minimum demands of the Catholic opposition, it was ten times more difficult for them to establish what the IRA would settle for. As the war dragged on into another year, and Protestants understandably demanded fiercer and fiercer measures against the terrorism which made Belfast a decaying city, and British troops were step by step allowed to take those measures, and their resulting roughness with parts of the Catholic population only increased the mistrust on which the IRA grew fat, nothing was more certain than that it was the IRA with whom the British authorities must in the end do business (just as they had in 1921 with Sinn Fein, whom Lloyd George repeatedly denounced as 'the murder gang' until the moment of negotiation).

But there was no basis to begin on. The IRA was not merely a divided body: the leadership of both main divisions was shifting, partly anonymous, and operating at any rate on the propaganda front as much against each other as against the forces of order: it was also an actively dissident body, beside which members of the parliamentary opposition were pillars of the established order. A government neither had nor could have direct lines to it. This was true even of the Government of Ireland, in spite of the fact that their long-term aim of a united Ireland coincided to some extent with the IRA's own. After Charles Haughey and Neil Blaney were dismissed from Jack Lynch's Cabinet in May 1970, and Kevin Boland left it in sympathy, there was no-one left in it who had even unofficial contacts with the IRA.

In this pre-negotiatory period there could be no messengers between the two sides but reporters, through their reporting. For the most part they took on the role unwittingly. Those of them who wrote about Northern Ireland could talk to the British ministers concerned. The conversations would be 'for use, but not for attribution': the reporter could record what ministers thought, but not how he knew, thus leaving open the possibility that the source was an official of theirs or even sheer invention: no minister was engaged. It meant that their views were to some extent strained through the reporter's own prejudgments about what was possible or desirable. But the IRA leaders were assiduous newspaper readers, and had some knowledge of the prejudgments of individual journalists to help them decode the signal.

The signal travelling in the other direction was even more overt. IRA country was not North Vietnam, where few journalists were admitted beyond proven sympathisers. For some time IRA leaders seemed prepared to talk to almost any known journalist who asked to talk to them, and quite often for quotation. During the week in August 1971 when the forces of order in Belfast rounded up hundreds of suspected terrorists for internment, the IRA held a press conference there – partly to indicate that at any rate some of its leaders were still at large.

More usually they saw journalists without this degree of bravado, in ones and twos. The meeting could be arranged with rather less fuss than a visit to a British general. Indeed, I remember the sense that it was unreally and callously easy as I sat in the back kitchen of a house on the edge of a small town in the Irish Midlands and talked, at a time of insistent and murderous violence in Belfast, to a man who bore much of the responsibility both for devising and justifying it. The sense of unrelatedness to real events was heightened by his own chilling cheeriness, his manner of discussing killings and explosions like a schoolmaster giving a common-room account of a playground scrap. We talked by the light of a single candle; but that followed from a power strike, not from a concern with security. The man was readily reachable. A reporter from *The Times* telephoned while I was there. The receiver had to be held at arm's length: something in the way the telephone was tapped made the volume extraordinarily loud, and the voice of *The Times* thundered and crackled round the candle-lit kitchen.

If the Irish authorities could tap the man's telephone, they could of course have arrested him. They knew where he was. They made no such attempt. If they had, they could only (short of internment, which the British experience made look inadvisable) have proceeded against him for membership of an illegal organisation, and they could only have got a conviction on the evidence of journalists, the only people outside his own association to whom he admitted membership. If that evidence was ever given, IRA men would not be able to entrust themselves to journalists again; and the only convenient channel between the IRA and the authorities would be blocked. The war might then go on even longer than it need, for lack of means to begin negotiations.

Governments do not formulate these things to themselves in so many words. They should: it might deliver them from the kind of error which both the British and Irish Governments began increasingly to fall into. Twice in 1971 the Irish Government committed itself to moves against journalists whose actions might keep the channel open. In September the Government allowed a Prohibition of Forcible Entry and Occupation Bill to pass into law with a clause in it directed against the 'encouragement' of squatting (a form of largely social protest favoured by certain IRA sympathisers) and drawn widely enough to cover newspaper reporting of it – though the young Minister of Justice finally agreed to amend that part of the bill at some future date. And in October Mr. Lynch used his powers under the Republic's Broadcasting Act to ask Radio Telefis Eireann 'to refrain from broadcasting any material that could be calculated to promote the aims or activities of any organisation engaged in violence to achieve political ends' – which meant no more interviews with IRA men.

True, IRA activists seemed just as blind to the strategic usefulness of an unintimidated press. That same month, production of a number of Dublin newspapers was stopped by a strike of delivery drivers: their vans had been so often attacked in the North that they were demanding danger money for going there. And these were papers with a certain sympathy for IRA aims.

The United Kingdom authorities showed no greater wisdom. In April 1971 they subpoenaed a BBC television reporter, Bernard Falk, to give evidence in a Belfast court in the case of a suspected terrorist. Asked whether the accused was the same man as an acknowledged Provisional whom he had interviewed (unidentifiably) for *24 Hours*, Mr. Falk refused to say. He wanted it understood that journalists could keep a secret. He was sent to prison for four days. Yet his resolution was put to no use. That interview was one of the last with an active IRA sympathiser which the BBC high command sanctioned that year; and BBC reporters were told to tell IRA people whom they interviewed that 'all information conveyed would be passed on to the police'.

Very few reporters thrust themselves into the office of semaphore between two warring sides. They do their ordinary job, seeking out the people who are in control of events and asking them the questions that their readers and audiences would like answered; and if that makes them helpful or unhelpful, it is not a part they chose. That seems to me to be a right stance. I very much doubt whether it is the journalist's business, as a reporter, to give events a push. It is his business, when he is serving as a journalist of opinion, to try to influence decisions; but that is a rather different thing.

There are nevertheless always grey areas, awkward decisions, even crises of what in other trades might be called conscience. In June 1971 a very senior British army officer in Northern

Ireland explained to me why soldiers objected to the idea of interning suspected terrorists and then suggested to me that it would be helpful if journalists did not write about internment for a while, since when the army finally took the step they would be more likely to find their men at home if there had been a lull in speculation about it. This seemed to me fair evidence of what later proved to be the case, that the army already foresaw that they would soon have to yield to political pressure and intern. If they had to do it, they wanted to do it as effectively as possible.

Journalists are disciplined receivers of requests not to write about things: it is the basis on which they get a lot of information, and a journalist who systematically flouts such requests may find information increasingly hard to get. It was also clear that a news story about the army foreseeing internment would be of the non-self-fulfilling kind, since the army would not be able to move until any resulting restlessness had died down. And there seemed nothing to be gained from gratuitously making life more difficult for British soldiers than it already was. On those counts, I reported nothing about the likelihood of internment. Yet perhaps I should have done. The Sunday before and the Sunday after the internment sweep was made, in August, my paper pointed out in its leader columns that internment was morally as well as practically objectionable; and (in my role as a journalist of opinion) I agreed with that view, and helped sustain it.

If I had really wanted to prevent internment, I should have predicted it as often as I could. That at any rate was the un-hesitating view of a group of American students to whom I mentioned the quandary a few weeks later. I saw their point, but I was not convinced. Deliberately interventionist reporting is very little distance away from wishful reporting and even knowingly false reporting.

On a warm evening in May 1968, Paris students were building barricades near the Luxembourg Gardens. It was more than a revolutionary reflex: after several weeks of argument with the authorities and the police about the state of French society in general and French higher education in particular they had stopped going to lectures: the police had promptly occupied the Sorbonne buildings of the university, and the students were intent on setting up an armed camp of their own over against it. There seemed no possibility of contact between the two sides.

A little before ten in the evening, the Rector of the Sorbonne announced that he was prepared to talk about a return to work. The announcement was the lead story on Radio Luxembourg's ten o'clock news bulletin. A good many students heard it: they had transistor radios propped on window-ledges beside them as they man-handled uprooted paving-stones into place; and as a source of news they preferred Radio Luxembourg – the name comes from the Grand Duchy where the transmitters are, not from the Gardens – to the state channels of the ORTF. More than that, a Radio Luxembourg reporter haled one of the three student leaders, Alain Geismar, to a microphone in a radio car. He explained that the students did not simply want to go back to work: they wanted the police out, and their friends out of police hands or out of prison.

Whether or not the Rector was listening, the Vice-Rector was. He telephoned the broadcasting station: a connection was made, and he found himself – by agreement – talking to the student leader, with their conversation broadcast. He declared himself ready to come down to the barricades and talk. But about what: the Rector's offer, or the students' newly clarified and wider wishes? The Vice-Rector would have to check with the Minister of Education: he would have an answer in a few minutes. Fair enough, said Alain Geismar; and if all the people who live in the Latin Quarter put their transistor sets on their window-sills, all the students would hear the Minister's answer.

When it came, after some thirty minutes, it was an anticlimax: discussion could only be about going back to work. The Minister of Education, Alain Peyrefitte, had decided on a hard line; and when the Prime Minister, Georges Pompidou, got back from Afghanistan the following evening and reversed the decision, he was too late. Another night of fierce rioting brought the unions in, a general strike was called, and campus politics were left behind. *Les événements* were in course. But the opportunity had been there. A news organisation, taking its chances, had supplied the authorities with up-to-date information about the state of mind of the people who for the moment led the domestic opposition.

Journalists can do the same service for more orthodox oppo-sitions, though oppositions themselves are not always aware of it. In conventional politics, out-parties always want as much attention from journalists as they can get. But that is chiefly as a means, they hope, to regaining power as a government: the demands for equal time, for the same volume of attention as is given to the Government, grow shriller as elections draw nearer. An out-party sometimes forgets that the power it exercises as an opposition, at any rate in a democratic system, is to some extent in the hands of journalists.

At the Labour Party conference at Brighton in October 1971, Harold Wilson, the Leader of the Opposition, was indignant at newspaper correspondents for the way they reported the con-ference debate about Britain and the Common Market – in which Mr. Wilson himself spoke. It resulted in a five-to-one vote against entry; yet the press seemed at least as interested in the private tally kept by a few Labour MPs of how many among them would vote with the Conservative Government in favour of entry when the matter came to the push in Parliament. The press was right in its emphasis, all the same. Although Labour had been Marketeers in office, they were already known to be anti-Marketeers in opposition: the change brought them more in tune with the party's natural insularity and the apparent state of public opinion. What mattered now was the effect which their anti-Market sentiment would have on the Government.

Oppositions like to suppose that the influence they have on governments is wielded in Parliament, either through argument across the floor of the House and in committee or by negotiation through the usual channels, which is the parliamentary euphem-ism for the whips' offices. But at least as usual a channel for influence is the press. Journalists do not enjoy an opposition's whole confidence, but they enjoy more of it than the govern-ment does. They are thus better able than the government to distinguish between what opposition members say they will do and what they will in fact do. This was a crucial piece of know-ledge for the Government's business managers in formulating their own shifting plans for the parliamentary management of the Market argument. They could best get it from the press.

The issue before MPs at the end of that October, and which they resolved by deciding for Europe, was a simple one. The

Six's offer was known: Britain could take it or leave it: there was not much more bargaining to be done. But there are many instances where, even within a chosen line, considerable modifications are possible. This is an area where a parliamentary opposition ought to be particularly valuable; and it often is. Government bills are regularly improved by painstaking opposition criticism in committee. But opposition is a difficult business. Opposition politicians have found themselves handicapped in it by sloth, the need to make a living outside Parliament, the absence of expert help, or the difficulty of finding public fault with proposals which they had themselves favoured when last in office. Here again, journalists help. As between the opposition and the press, said a senior civil servant who had worked closely with a Labour Foreign Secretary and a Conservative Prime Minister, 'governments are inclined to regard the press as their more effective and persistent critic'.

This was notably true of the main legislative achievement of the Heath Government in its first session, the Industrial Relations Act. Labour's opposition – like their opposition to Market entry – was fatally damaged by the fact that they had backed a very similar move when they were themselves in power, though Labour's plans for trade union reform had roused a degree of union disquiet which made a change of mind in opposition hard to avoid. Labour even put forward the same front-bench spokesman, Barbara Castle – at her own self-exculpatory insistence – to attack what she had previously defended. In these circumstances the Conservative Government could not be expected to take its ordained opponents seriously. But the gap in opposition was to some extent filled by the press. A number of newspapers followed the bill in detail through its committee stage, drawing on expert opinion: a number of the changes made in the bill had been suggested in newspaper comment.

Press argument tallied with official argument within the Department of Employment and Productivity, and civil servants would sometimes produce newspaper leaders to reinforce the points they were putting to ministers. But sometimes officials fail to put the counter-arguments. Indeed, a notorious difficulty of the Whitehall system is that it offers a minister not a choice of policies but a single policy, with all the senior officials of his ministry committed to defending it. Mr. Heath set up a Central

Policy Review Staff to overcome that very problem – to tell cabinet ministers, more authoritatively than their own departments could, what other choices were available to their colleagues besides the ones they actually brought to Cabinet for approval. Again, it was a task which was more easily discharged by the press; and there were cases – like the decision to site the third London airport at Stansted in Essex – where it was solely discharged by the press, until a change of minister in August 1967 compelled a departmental reappraisal. In that instance, once again, news organisations did their proper work of publicising views which were opposed to existing arrangements.

CHAPTER 6

A Link with the Governed

When Anthony Wedgwood Benn became Postmaster General in the first Wilson Government and wanted to explain to his staff what the new administration's aims for the Post Office were, he concluded that the easiest way to do it was to hire the Albert Hall. (He got the idea from Sir Stafford Cripps, who had hired the Central Hall, Westminster, early in the first Attlee Government to address the staff of the Board of Trade.) Any large department of state or public corporation presents the same problem: the right hand has grave difficulty in discovering what the left hand is up to. Failing the Albert Hall, news organisations can help. The officials of any large public body will scan the newspapers, in particular, for word of what is going on not just in the world around them but in other parts of their own concern.

Newspapers and news broadcasts are undoubtedly one of the means by which one part of central government learns what is happening or what might happen in another, and by which local government learns what is happening in central government. They give MPs some of their information and ideas. Backbench MPs regularly find subjects for questions in the press: indeed, it is not uncommon for a reporter to suggest a subject for questions to an MP, in order to strengthen his report with the news that a question is to be asked in the House about it. For events which fall somewhere between history and actuality, MPs are used to regarding newspapers as their chief source. When the *News Chronicle* closed in 1960, its library of newspaper cuttings went to the House of Commons.

Our governors have many other sources of information, though, about what has happened or is happening in government. The Vote Office, a mullioned window in the members' lobby of the Commons, dispenses it to MPs by the armful: records of debates, order papers, select committee findings, government white papers, drafts of bills, reports of nationalised bodies, and so on. The executive has its own more private and even more voluminous system for circulating papers.

The governed, on the other hand, are without all this. They are largely dependent, for their knowledge of what government is up to, on journalists.

If it is lucky, or overbearing, a government can use at any rate part of the work of journalists simply as a mouthpiece, presenting its views without inconvenient objections and without much notice of rival activities or comments. That was how the ORTF seemed to read its function during the de Gaulle years. Its view of news began to change after he left office; but as the new news director of its principal channel, Pierre Desgraupes, said to *L'Express* in July 1970: 'If a man has fallen into the habit of going to a government office every day to collect his orders, I know of no serum which can change his attitude overnight. Not even lion serum. And if I'd had some lion serum, and transformed one of these journalists, I'd still have to transform the man he goes to see as well; because if he'd seen the journalist suddenly coming on like a lion, he would have taken him for a lamb and kicked his bottom (*s'il l'avait vu tout d'un coup arriver en lion, il l'aurait pris pour un agneau et il lui aurait botté les fesses*).'

If it is less lucky, a government may find factual accounts of its words and deeds footnoted, in the press or on the air, with equally factual statements of the corresponding objections: that the promised bill cannot be law for another three years, that the new motorway still indicates a rate of road construction far slower than the rate of new car registration. These may come from an opponent of the government: they may come from the reporter himself. Government ministers value the uninterrupted ministerial broadcast, straight to camera, because it assures them not just of publication in full but of freedom from that kind of talk-back. American presidents seem to have found it especially precious. (The talk-back sometimes comes up all the same, if the broadcasting organisation arranges for studio comment to follow the great man's message – a practice which used to give rise to recurrent Washington arguments between the White House and the networks.)

Journalists are at least as active, though, in ferrying information in the opposite direction: from the governed to their governors. This is not necessarily state-of-the-nation stuff. Where the information is fact, it is as a rule specific fact. General fact – unemployment figures, housing statistics – is usually gathered by official agencies. Where it is opinion, it is often specific opinion, with a name attached. But governors are also extremely curious about general opinion, states of mind among people at large. Journalists take it as part of their task to meet this curiosity.

Few newspapers or broadcasting organisations would maintain that actual audience participation is much use for the purpose. Letters to the editor, phoned-in contributions to telethons or radio talk shows, are the preserve of the untypically self-confident or strong-minded; and they are chosen, where choice is possible, to be interesting rather than representative. Even the letters page of *The Times*, enlarged since September 1970 and unique in journalism as a notice-board for the great and good, is clearly edited not so much with a view towards giving a small minority of the paper's readers their opportunity for a public statement – they have plenty of others – as with a view towards entertaining the readers as a whole.

When W. T. Arnold, Matthew Arnold's nephew, toured Ireland early in 1880 for the *Manchester Guardian* to report on the condition of the people in a winter when the potato crop had failed, journalists were still bold enough to be their own sociologists. It was an important journey for the paper: it began the *Guardian*'s slow conversion to Irish Home Rule in parallel with Gladstone's. In thirteen long articles, Arnold drew on his own observations of how people lived, his own record of what they said. He was unabashed by any thought that what he saw and heard might not be representative: he backed his own judgment that it was. Reporters continued to use this method, without suspecting that there might be anything wrong with it, until about the time of the Second World War. Then two new instruments began to cast doubt on the usefulness of the old one: the social survey and the opinion poll.

Dr. George Gallup forecast his first American presidential election result in 1936. (It was not a difficult one: it was the beginning of President Franklin Roosevelt's second term, when he overwhelmed Governor Alfred Landon of Kansas by 523 electoral votes to 8.) The first opinion poll appeared in a British

newspaper, the *News Chronicle*, in 1937. Sociology made the
eastward crossing of the Atlantic less rapidly, but no less in-
exorably. It began to become established at European universities
after the Second World War (when the word sociology itself,
and the study, were already about a hundred years old); and in
Britain *New Society*, the weekly review which first brought some
of the findings within reach of ordinary journalists, was founded
late in 1962.

The slow consequence of these imports has been to make
journalists in Britain chary of social generalisation except on the
basis of other people's figures – of which the most comprehensive,
the results of the national census, are only collected in full every
ten years – and of electoral or political prediction except on the
basis of opinion polls. In successive general elections, more and
more attention was paid to opinion polls; and in the 1970 election, journalists made them their main focus of interest. At least
as much heed was paid to what the voters thought, or were
thought to think, as to what the candidates said. The lead story in
the *Sunday Times* was about opinion polls on each of the four
Sundays before polling day.

The result was an interesting débâcle. Of five opinion polls,
four gave as their final forecast a Labour victory; and the fifth,
Opinion Research Centre, only hazarded a narrow Conservative
win – narrower than it was in fact – as a result of a carefully
calculated guess at the amount by which zeal to vote among
Conservative supporters would exceed Labour zeal.

Even more interesting was the extreme brevity of the slump
in the standing of opinion polls among journalists. A year later
the debate about whether or not Britain should join the Common
Market was being conducted almost entirely in terms of opinion
poll findings. Mr. Heath had been unwise enough to undertake
not to lead Britain into the Market without the 'full-hearted
consent' of the British people, as if that were something which
could be clearly identified; and the claim that consent was barely
even half-hearted was much used by opponents of entry.

The responsibility for encouraging public men in these sim-
plicities lies with journalists. When they report opinion-poll
findings, journalists do not always explain as rigorously as they
should that sampling error may have distorted each side's real
score by 3 per cent, which could throw the gap between the two

sides out by 6 per cent; nor are they always scrupulous in ex-
plaining that, even if there is no sampling error, the results are
only valid for the time (perhaps a week ago) when the questions
were in fact asked. The pollsters themselves could of course
insist that these qualifying points should be made; and so they
do, retrospectively, whenever their judgments are proved wrong
by the hard arithmetic of an electoral result. But the pollsters
are uncomfortably aware that newspapers would not print, nor
broadcasters broadcast, propositions of the form: 'A week ago
the state of public opinion produced something between a 2 per
cent lead for Labour and a 4 per cent lead for the Conservatives';
and yet the pollsters like their work published, not least because
their bread and butter is in commercial market research – enquiries about whether people prefer their chocolate biscuits milk
or plain sometimes appear in the same list as the political questions – and they believe their political polls to be a useful advertisement for their firms. So journalists are allowed to go on
overplaying opinion poll results.

On more complicated questions than voting intention, there
is a more serious difficulty. It is that pollsters cannot help eliciting
opinions which are sometimes held lightly or not at all. Even on
a much discussed issue, like Britain and the Market, to have an
opinion requires an effort of mind, and one which – judged by
the impressionistic methods of the journalist – most people were
not disposed to make. They were content to leave the decision
to the Government. But they were not prepared to say so to the
pollsters: few people will cheerfully confess to opinionlessness.
So they summoned up the scrap of information they could most
easily grasp, which was in most cases the likely further rise in the
cost of food, and they evolved from it – on their own doorstep,
with their supper cooling behind them – an opinion they had
never owned till then.

On issues which have not been the subject of much public
discussion, this virtual fabrication of public opinion by the pollsters becomes an active absurdity. With commendable honesty,
Opinion Research Centre demonstrated this in a poll it ran in
April 1971. The issue chosen was the desirability of a referendum
on Market entry: it was a device which a few politicians who
foresaw the impossibility of changing Mr. Heath's mind by any
other means were beginning to advocate. Would it be a good

idea, ORC enquired of its sample of opinion, if the Government asked the people to vote yes or no before it decided whether we should go into the Common Market? Yes, a majority thought it would. But a majority also said – as each suggestion was put to them – that they would like the same motions gone through before MPs' pay was put up, before food prices were increased and before a wage freeze was imposed. It was an impressively consistent demand for more power to the people. But then a similar majority spoilt it all by saying that they thought important national decisions should be taken by the elected government rather than by the people.

The inescapable impression is of people prepared to hail anything that looks like a good idea as their own opinion. But such a measurement is strictly valueless. It does not mean that the body of opinion of which this is supposed to be a sample does in fact exist: it does not even mean that public agreement could be secured to the idea put forward, since it has been put forward by the pollsters (quite properly) without the due objections. Opinion Research Centre had intended to test the idea that public demand for a Market referendum was weak and thoughtless. The idea proved all too well founded. The result suggested the dangerous thought that almost any opinion discovered by a pollster might be weak and thoughtless too.

Surveys, treading more factual ground than polls, come up against another obstacle. Because a question is factual, the answer is not necessarily factual too. Jeremy Tunstall, an academic sociologist, compiled his entertaining book *Journalists at Work* from questionnaires sent to a number of specialist journalists, of whom I was one. The questions were all perfectly fair and sensible; but some of them were impossible to answer truthfully. How often did I call my newsdesk? I had absolutely no idea, without running a laborious exercise in self-observation over what might then turn out to be a quite untypical period. How many of my stories did I think up, and how many did my office? Most stories seemed to think of themselves: they simply happened. Did I make more telephone calls than I received? Well, probably; and yet it seemed such an acknowledgment of an unloved life that I was sorely tempted to fiddle the figures. Did I ever have to treat my news sources with deference? I would be reluctant to say so if I did. . . .

When Mr. Tunstall put the book together, he was clearly aware of such problems and kept them scrupulously in mind. The fact remains that, since the man answering this kind of questionnaire has to put something down, if only to get the thing off his desk, not all the answers are of the same degree of reliability.

Happily, even if the journalist is shy now of impressionistic evidence, surveys and opinion polls are not the only first-class source material available to him as he goes about the task of telling governments about the physical and mental condition of the governed. There remains the journalist himself. It is a commonplace of television or radio interviewing technique that the interviewer asks those questions which the ordinary intelligent and concerned citizen will want answered. How does he know what questions are in that citizen's mind? By looking into his own.

CHAPTER 7

Commission and Omission

If the journalist asks questions of government with the voice of his readers or listeners or viewers, then he ought in some sense to be like them. It is a matter of common complaint that he is not. He exhibits social and political biases which contrive to separate him from one group after another in the population which surrounds him.

Most journalists working for organs of mass communication can be said to be on the side of the established order. They would stop well short of the assertion that whatever is, is right; but much of their work shows a broad approval of the way things are arranged in their own country and of the standards current among people most disposed to accept that arrangement, together with a marked scepticism about alternative systems – particularly if they come from abroad.

That observation is not entirely cancelled out by the fact that journalists are also regularly attacked for exhibiting the opposite tendency. No journalist can expect to stand up in front of a Conservative audience without being made answerable for the shortcomings of all journalists, from making fun of anti-pornography crusaders to disrespectful editing of Conservative speeches. But this charge of iconoclasm, of cultural and political subversion, is not incompatible with the charge that journalists are forehead-knucklers in their hearts. To misapply the language of the Church, establishmentarianism and disestablishmentarianism can coexist in the same body. It is possible to believe in the natural inferiority of the working classes (without setting out the belief in so many words) and still supply them – in order to keep them contented in their cave – with an occasional dig at their betters. Popular organs do it a lot. One of the men who taught me the craft of writing commentaries for news film on commercial television used to take as his imaginary referee, his guide to the choice of phrase and illustration, a figure he called 'Mum in Wigan' – a name filled with the scorn felt for the uneducated by the half-educated; and Mum in Wigan was known to relish a little naughtiness, an occasional irreverence, as long as the context left no doubt that the Queen was still on her throne and the flag still flew.

Nor is it a total explanation of either tendency, towards conformism or towards irreverence, to say that they are both a natural consequence of literacy – that the educated mind recoils from extremes, whether of anarchism or reaction. The sad fact is that journalists, as a body, are not as literate as they would like to think. In any newspaper on any day you can find examples of words misused (*pristine* to mean *shining* instead of *ancient*, *hopefully* to mean *I hope* instead of *in hope*) and commas left out ('Mr. Barber, the Chancellor of the Exchequer said last night . . .'): the immediate effect is to impede understanding, and the slow effect is to lessen the language's precision and versatility.

Unmeditated metaphor abounds. On the day I write this paragraph a well-known freelance columnist in *The Times*, with plenty of time to write carefully, takes a 'sudden evaporation of interest' to mean that an issue has 'come off the boil'. Sudden evaporation more ordinarily follows from staying on the boil. On the same day, a well-known columnist in the *Guardian* discusses a quarrel between an MP and his constituency party: three times (until it is put right in the last edition) the wrong town is named. Accuracy, of phrase and fact, is not an unfailing commodity even at the top of the trade. And a mistake made in nine-point type will be acknowledged – if at all – in much smaller six-point type.

'OH, ENGLAND, ENGLAND!' The *Daily Mirror*'s huge page-one headline, ten days before polling in the June 1970 general election, was not a lament for the falling standard of political debate. The England football team had lost to Brazil in the World Cup by a single goal. The next day, though, the *Mirror* turned back to the election in what the paper thought were the terms that mattered: 'Man for man, who would you put YOUR money on?' The question was developed over the next few issues of the paper in paired studies of leading people in both main parties. 'Who do you want on your side in a crisis?

Unruffled Jim – or Excitable Quintin? Cool-it Callaghan or Hot-beneath-the-collar Hogg?'

Determined triviality, deliberate personalisation – the failings are not hard to document; and they are less excusable in print than on the television screen, where the need for pictures sometimes enjoins them. To them is often added a preoccupation with violence, or with any situation that gives promise of it. No eggs were so much counted as the ones thrown at Harold Wilson during that campaign. Demonstrations are another draw. They are mounted to demonstrate belief: what brings journalists out is not the belief but the chance that there will be a rough encounter with unbelievers or the police.

Besides what might be called social biases of that kind, there is also old-fashioned political bias to be reckoned with. The long-heard Labour cry about Britain's Tory press has a certain force. By one method of reckoning, the national press is evenly balanced between the two main parties. If you add together the circulations of the national newspapers which declared in the June 1970 general election for one party or the other, and count daily papers six times for a Sunday paper's once, then the two sides show remarkable symmetry. Some fifty-seven million papers a week were being sold on each side of the argument. But that simple sum leaves several considerations out of account.

First, it omits provincial morning and Sunday papers, which are almost uniformly Conservative. More important, Labour papers only declared their decision towards the end of the campaign: except for the *Sunday Times*, the ones that came out for the Conservatives made very little secret of their allegiance from the start. There were three tabloid dailies then in existence. Of these, the *Sketch* was the first national daily paper to give its readers advice on how to vote, with exactly a month still to run before polling day. 'If the choice is between Happy Harold's half-hour on TV and a return to honest government at Westminster . . . we know where we'd put our X on the ballot paper.' The next day the *Mirror* and the *Sun*, in leaders which they ran as their lead stories, both made it clear that the party which was to get their endorsement would have to wait for it. The *Mirror* wrote: 'This newspaper will give a fair show to each political side. . . . When the time comes, nearer polling day, . . . the *Mirror* won't be sitting on the fence. You will be hearing from us loud and clear.' And the *Mirror's* sworn rival: 'The *Sun* has a mind of its own – like you. We will speak our mind.' They both kept their nerve, and their counsel, when a prospective newspaper stoppage (which in fact lasted four days) made it seem that their issue nine days before polling would be their last of the campaign; and they only spoke their minds in the end, for Labour, with a day to go.

Conservative newspapers did not simply pin their hearts to their sleeves earlier than Labour: they also let their enthusiasm seep out of their leader columns and into their news columns. Unfair things are said on both sides in any election: the Conservatives were better supplied than Labour with newspapers prepared to stress the unfair things said on their side and omit the awkward things, while making as much as they could of the flashes of truthfulness on the other side. The *Daily Express* used a rhetorical prediction of Edward Heath's about 'the three-shilling loaf' (the price was then a little over half that) as a main front-page headline: it reported a speech of Quintin Hogg's about Enoch Powell, an *Express* hero for his low view of black immigration, without carrying the crucial sentence 'The Conservative party does not support Mr. Powell'; and a mild observation by James Callaghan to the effect that a Labour government would have to 'give attention' to wage increases after the election was greeted with a page-one shout of 'Callaghan lets it out: new pay freeze threat'. Parallel examples were to be found in the *Daily Mail*.

Public men have sometimes had the idea that the antidote to this kind of partiality is the impartiality of broadcasters, secured not so much by the camera's inability to lie (in which there are few believers left) as by the extent to which broadcasters are open to political bullying. Impartiality is then indeed secured, but at the expense of pungency. The 1970 general election furnished an impressive volume of examples. ITN's *News at Ten*, the longest and most watched news programme on television, was displaced by party commercials (with the happy connivance of the BBC, which also had to carry them) on thirteen out of the last sixteen weekday evenings of the campaign. The Conservatives added parody to larceny by casting their own commercials in very much the same form as *News at Ten*. Using the fact that under the Representation of the People Act 1969 the withdrawal of any one party's spokesman from an election programme meant the programme's collapse, the parties were able to veto the BBC's most cherished election project – two-and-a-half-hour courtroom examinations of each party's policies. They had no difficulty in stopping reports on any constituency (and there were several) where any party had a candidate which embarrassed it, nor in imposing a virtual ban on any programme which risked bringing politicians into contact with actual voters. Harold Wilson succeeded in imposing his choice of anodyne interviewer on both ITV and BBC at the beginning of the campaign, and in dictating his own choice of party spokesman and therefore of subject to the BBC's *Panorama* at the end.

To these enforced absurdities the broadcasters added one or two of their own. Even before the campaign began an ITV company, Thames, withdrew an episode of a popular thriller serial because it was about an attempt on the life of a politician with certain similarities to Enoch Powell; and the BBC suppressed an item on an arts programme about Edward Heath as an organist. During the four-day newspaper stoppage in the middle of the campaign itself, the rigidity of commercial programming meant that only the BBC could lengthen its news and current affairs coverage; and the time was given over to unsynthesised outside opinion rather than to any additional analysis of the news by the BBC's own specialist reporters.

Television had its industrial misfortunes as well as newspapers. Granada, another ITV company, had intended to wall up a hundred voters in a hall of residence at Leeds University and bombard them with political television of a quite untypical rigour. The hundred would have been exposed to largely academic lectures which gave the fullest information possible on each of ten issues: only then would they have been laid open to the rhetoric of party spokesmen. The lectures would themselves have been broadcast, albeit to small midday audiences; and the hundred subjects would have had their voting intentions tested before and after each stage, to see if either fact or argument made any difference. But Granada had a technicians' strike, and the experiment was called off.

Broadcasting's feebleness at election time is only part of a larger phenomenon: systematic sins of omission by news organisations in general. There are a number of wide open spaces where the journalist treads rarely. Foreign affairs is in danger of becoming one such, even for newspapermen. No British newspaper can now claim to be a journal of record for even the principal events in even the foreign countries most important to Britain, like America or France; and newspapers and broadcasting organisations turn more and more to a figure who should have died with the thirties, the fit-all foreign correspondent. He jets from trouble-spot to trouble-spot, equipped with little besides a portable typewriter and a serviceable turn of phrase: his principal sources are taxi-drivers, barmen and other fit-all foreign correspondents. British staff journalists abroad dwindle all the time; and there are several capitals where the day-to-day interests of British readers and viewers are very patchily served. A few years ago I was approached by a Greek in Addis Ababa – not the least active diplomatic capital in Africa – who showed me a card which seemed to indicate that almost every newspaper in London regarded him as their local correspondent. On nights when there was news in Addis, the paper which paid him the least generous retainer must have had to wait a little while for word.

Even at home, there are large tracts of government where a journalist is a rare sight. Whitehall is largely unwatched: the doings of ministers are regularly brought into the open, but their officials ply their trade in private. And what is true of Whitehall is truer still of town halls and local government offices, where even the doings of elected representatives are to a great extent unscanned. Admission to council committee meetings has been a right much demanded by local newspapers. One council which lets the press in is at Weston-super-Mare. In September 1971 a long meeting of the council's finance and general purposes committee passed 49 minutes on matters like local government reorganisation, capital expenditure and rural bus services. Yet the only two items which the local evening paper thought fit to print dealt with a staff social club ('Civil servants' rest room', said the headline) and a lavatory for the information bureau ('It's such relief').

Even if the whole of government were well reported, there would still be a lacuna in the coverage of public affairs. The gap is dissent. Journalists are better at reporting the fact than the matter of protest. The antics of the unilateral nuclear disarmers were always better copy than their arguments – to the point where journalists must bear some of the responsibility for the fact that their arguments are now so little heard. Trade unionists have often voiced something of the same complaint. A report prepared by the union which covers technicians in television itself, ACTT, pointed out that BBC television news went right through an evening of long reports on a day of protest against the Industrial Relations Bill in January 1971 without any interviews to elicit the views of protesters. The political fringes – anything to the left or right of those two great coalitions of the centre, the Labour and Conservative parties – are seldom written about now by political correspondents: they get their mentions, if they get any at all, from the gossip columnists.

The young, perhaps the most notable omission, are heard from hardly at all; or if they are, in last year's slang, and patronisingly.

It is no sufficient answer to say that the alternative society is reported by its own alternative system of communication, the underground press. The trouble with the underground press is that it is largely unread. The name suggests smudged sheets passed furtively from hand to hand behind the backs of the police. In fact its papers can be bought at any bookstall which cares to carry them. But they are not bought. 'Idiot International has collapsed, Black Dwarf is dormant, the bailiff is at IT's door, Friends flails valiantly. . . .' The list is from a 1971 editorial in *Oz*. It is a striking echo of a 1712 letter of Jonathan Swift's to Stella, when he told her that Grub Street was dead: 'The Observator is fallen, the Medleys are jumbled together with the Flying-post, the Examiner is deadly sick. . . .' But that was the effect of a new newspaper duty in the Stamp Act. The modern Grub Street's problem looks much more like a plain failure of professionalism. The barely legible typography, with coloured print plastered on top of coloured pictures; the insistent use of a few short and ugly words, whether or not they fit the sense; the fascination with a very narrow range of experience, returning again and again to pop music and drugs: all this argues an indifference to the reader. That its chosen public does not read the underground press is perhaps no great matter. The sad thing is that it is unreadable by the very people who need to read it. The conformist world needs to be made aware how the noncomformist world thinks and lives, and these papers cannot do it. The message is hardly to be deciphered even by journalists. So the gap in news from the alternative society remains.

The common point in all these gaps is that available knowledge is not drawn upon – about the administration of national and local affairs, about people whose views are not heard within the ordinary processes of government. The citizen's oldest complaint against journalists is that as soon as they report on anything he knows about, they get it wrong. This is partly the natural man's instinct to make a mystery of his own speciality, and to contest the notion that anyone can learn in a day or two what it has taken him years to master; but the general scepticism which it suggests has a grounding in truth. Specialist knowledge is the great scarcity. Advances in scholarship, or in the multitudinous disciplines which now subsist on the borders of scholarship, risk going unrecorded. Discoveries stand their best chance of being disinterred from specialist journals if they are amusing (as that toothpaste is after all no use) or ghoulish (as that the end of the world is at hand).

There is a body of people who make a living by claiming that they can overcome, for a fee, this tendency among journalists to leave uncovered what they ought to have covered. These people are public relations men: flaks, in a useful Washington coinage. (Flak came to mean anti-aircraft fire as the acronym of a long German compound. William Safire, in his dictionary *The New Language of Politics*, traces the transference to the fact that anti-aircraft shells emit smoke puffs and public relations men verbal puffs.) Where the flak's task is to secure coverage for a motor-car or a holiday resort in a form which is in effect unpaid advertising, he can sometimes manage it – though it often happens that, by an arrangement which does credit neither to the newspaper nor to the advertiser, paid advertising for the same client is to be found close by. Where the problem is to secure coverage for events or opinions which might otherwise go unnoticed, the flak is a good deal less successful, notably in the world of politics and public affairs. That is why senior politicians in London are undisturbed by the number of junior politicians who become flaks in order to eke out their salary as MPs: their activities have very little effect on the course of journalism, let alone the course of events. This becomes a shadier area when flaks are in effect lobbyists, and seek to secure not so much press interest as government interest in some cause: commercial broadcasting, or friendship with the régime in Greece.

The trade survives because many things to which flaks draw journalists' attention do in fact get published, and no-one can ever demonstrate that the flak's action was wholly irrelevant. He capitalises on this uncertainty. He cannot show his client a list of journalists whose intentions he has changed, but he can produce a list of journalists to whom he sent a press release or a party invitation. Much of his activity, in short, is an exercise in justifying his fee.

The reef which flaks founder on is the powerful distrust which most journalists entertain for them. Since many flaks are journalists who have for one reason and another left journalism, journalists tend to regard them as failures or deserters. This is less strongly felt about the staff of Whitehall press offices, even where they are ex-journalists, because their role is a comparatively neutral one: they pass out documents and answer questions, usually on a basis of no greater information than has already been published. Perhaps journalists recognise that they are themselves toilers in the same vineyard, although with different loyalties. Or perhaps they simply need the information.

CHAPTER 8

The Terms of the Trade

Journalists' sins of commission and omission cannot be argued away. They happen every week. There are none the less certain reasons, external to journalists, why those sins and not others should preponderate; and before deciding which are remediable and which are not, it is worth setting the reasons out. One group arises from the given technical and economic needs of news journalism: the other from the nature of politics itself.

A notable feature of the world of journalism is the haphazardry of it. This is another reason why public relations is a barren exercise: chance plays so large a part in journalists' decisions that even the most cunning plans to sway them are in danger of being frustrated at the last. The most important influences in determining what items are to be reported, and with what emphasis, are again and again the banal accidents of time and space.

Much ink and indignation is expended on the question of why journalists choose to present some happenings for notice and not others. In October 1971 the *Sunday Times* reported sworn and detailed charges about the way IRA suspects detained or interned under the Special Powers Act were being questioned at a barracks outside Belfast. The story aroused a national furore. Many people were distressed at the thought that it might be true. Some people were indignant that it should have been published at all, when the charges were for the most part made by sympathisers with the state's enemies, and when comparable charges had been published two months before and were now being officially investigated (by Sir Edmund Compton and two colleagues).

The earlier charges reported in the British press had been of physical cruelty. The *Sunday Times* story was of cruelty calculated to upset the balance of prisoners' minds, perhaps permanently. The paper's Insight unit had in fact heard allegations in that

sense, made in prison to lawyers, soon after the August internment sweep. But then a number of accidents intervened. Check-
ing the story against what could be learnt of British army practice
elsewhere took time. A small girl was killed by gunmen firing
on an army patrol in a busy street: published then, the story ran
the risk of being read as a plea for civilised conduct towards a
body of men who had no notion of it themselves. It was decided
that the better course would be to set the new charges in context
by making them a part of a long article, then in preparation,
about the whole nature of Britain's re-involvement in the Irish
wars. The long article thereupon took on a life of its own, and
needed more time: it appeared later as two long articles, and later
still as a book. A dragging industrial dispute further complicated
the planning of large blocks of space in the paper.

Before all this was resolved, the interrogation story was an old
one, and there seemed no good reason to dwell on it except in
terms of fresh fact. Then on a Friday morning in mid-October
I happened to make two phone calls from London to two rural
addresses in Northern Ireland in pursuit of quite another story:
progress by the Northern Ireland Government with new political
reform plans, then overdue, and their likely effect on Catholic
attitudes. The army had recently been pulling in men and weapons
at a rate which suggested that they knew more than they used
to, and both men I spoke to brought up the subject of interrogation. One of them, a member of the Northern Ireland Cabinet
in a position to know, said that interrogation was producing
results – 'Those fellows are singing like hell' – and parried questions about method in a way which suggested reticence rather
than ignorance. The other, an Opposition MP with a Catholic
priest in his constituency who had been compiling interrogation
stories, spoke of 'totally unacceptable' goings-on at a named
barracks.

That afternoon I went over to Northern Ireland and found
that, besides the army's surge of arrests and arms finds, there was
another new element. A few men who claimed to have been
harshly questioned were beginning to be let out. I met one of
them in the headmaster's study of a Catholic seminary in County
Tyrone; and there I was also given a fresh sheaf of statements
made in prison by men who said they had been the victims not
just of physical but of psychological attack – bags over heads,

strange noises, and the rest of the miserable ritual which later became familiar. These accounts dated back to August, and might not of themselves have been a reason to reopen the affair, although the methods they described had not been reported in Britain.

But the crucial accident was that another young man had telephoned the *Sunday Times* newsdesk that afternoon from Belfast to say that he had been questioned and released only three days before. That evening he told our Belfast stringer his experiences in full. He was a second-year student of history and economics at Queen's University. His account did not complain of the same resourcefulness in mental cruelty as the prison statements did – though the methods he described, the strenuous attempts to induce bewilderment and despair, were alarming enough as used against a very young man whose questioners could find so little fault with him that they let him out again within thirty-six hours. But his narrative was by far the most recent to come to light and the most lucidly detailed. In particular he was positive about the place where he had been questioned, both because he knew the specific locality and because he was carried to and fro with less hugger-mugger than previous prisoners. As evidence, let alone as journalism, this was important. The cruelties complained of now had a local habitation: Palace Barracks, Holywood. And they were continuing.

It seemed to me, collating all this in the leader-writers' room of the *Belfast Telegraph* next morning, a Saturday, that there were now enough new elements for the charges to be reported as a news story, and that because of their *prima facie* credibility – a number of accounts concurred and yet could not all have been concerted – they deserved to be reported in order that they could be further examined: if they were true, they were striking and perhaps worrying evidence of what the effort to defeat an urban guerrilla enemy by military means alone now apparently entailed.

When this material arrived in London on Saturday afternoon (tapped out by a highly sceptical Protestant telex operator in Belfast), it was recognised as carrying further, and yet needing the support of, the older unpublished material. This was accordingly added from Insight files: it included further graphic detail of the techniques used, and the vital corroborative point that these techniques were in fact taught at a named army camp in Sussex. In that form the report was published: the day after publication the Prime Minister met the Leader of the Opposition and the shadow Home Secretary to discuss it, and a month later the truth of the charges was substantially upheld by the Compton report.

Late on that same Saturday afternoon, a British soldier was shot and killed in Londonderry. Army headquarters in Belfast, acting on their normal rules, kept back his name and the name of his unit until his nearest relatives had been told of his death: no Derry journalist appeared to have been near the scene at the time, and from Belfast it was too late to set enquiries on foot for next morning's paper. Accordingly there was almost nothing to report except that a soldier had been killed while the army was dispersing a crowd in a certain part of the city, and that he was the 26th to die in Northern Ireland that year. The story was on the front page of the paper, but it only filled ten lines; whereas the Palace Barracks story filled a column on page one and two more on page two. A reader wrote to protest against the scale of values indicated in that comparison. In fact it indicated nothing except a long chain of chances about what information came to hand and what did not.

Many of the chances of the trade are concerned, as in any activity, with its given technical needs. Its practitioners have to work to certain imperatives and in a certain medium. That medium, even for television journalists, is principally words. Words cannot be manipulated by illiterates. Clearly literacy is a scarce national resource like any other; and local newspapers or broadcasting stations will get less than their fair share of it in Britain, given the sad magnetism of the capital. (They will get less than their fair share even of that practical understanding of public affairs which comes with experience, since of those of their staff who acquire it a proportion will carry it too away with them to London.) Further, literacy – even the moderate degree of it found among journalists – is likely to accompany certain habits of mind. Work done on the social and educational origins of journalists is bound to discover that most of them come from homes and schools where they have learnt, in a more or less full sense, to read and write. If that pulls them away from political extremes, then the reflection is on extremism more than on literacy. That kind of origin is as much a dictate of the business in hand as is the fact that jockeys are not recruited from among fat men, nor construction workers from among men with no head for heights. The limitation is at any rate even-handed. It is no more favourable to the inarticulate extremism of the far right (where Lord Salisbury's phrase 'too clever by half' about one of the most thoughtful and humane men then in the Conservative Party, Iain Macleod, was received as a trenchant condemnation) than to the inarticulate extremism of the far left (where the emphasis laid by Eastern creeds like Zen on an absence of speech is gratefully taken to excuse an absence of thought). To that extent, certainly, journalists cannot suit all their clients.

Words, then, are a tool of the trade, and one whose use entails certain consequences. Pictures are another. Newspapers use pictures; but in newspaper offices they are chiefly prized by layout men, who see them as a way of rendering great expanses of print acceptable to the eye. Everyone knows that *Le Monde* is the worthiest newspaper in Europe: what also makes it the most difficult to finish is that it has no pictures. To television, on the other hand, pictures are meat and drink; and since its preferred diet is moving pictures, and nothing in the field of real events moves so impressively as a military force or an unruly crowd in action, television in particular sometimes shows a preoccupation with war and disorder.

Besides the requirements of words and pictures, which are not in themselves dead things, journalists have also to meet the imperatives of time and space. Time is incessantly demanding. The fact of regular publication – weekly, daily or more often – makes it hard to present as news things which are not new since last publication: this operates to the advantage of the swift single event, which may be trivial, and to the disadvantage of the slow current of events, which may be important. It also means that some journalists have to work fast all the time and all journalists have to work fast some of the time, which is the greatest single cause of inaccuracy: a comparison between the first and last editions of a morning paper, or between early and late takes of a news agency story, shows that extra time makes for at least some extra correctness.

More than that, the gathering speed of communication has

increased the pace at which editorial decisions must be made without increasing the wisdom available to make them. For the first twenty-five years of the *Manchester Guardian*'s life, until about 1847, the national and international news of the day would arrive at its offices in a lump, when the principal coach or train arrived from London; and its staff could proceed in measured fashion to lay out a circumscribed quantity of news to the best advantage. The electric telegraph changed all that. It brought more news, and it brought it more often, so that plans had to be constantly changed even while the paper was being produced. Something of the same happened, over a shorter time, to television news. When Independent Television News began broadcasting in 1955, the organisation seldom had more than enough news film to fill a ten-minute news bulletin, and its chief sources were an American syndicated package and what its own cameramen could get within reach of London. Inside twelve years the growth of jet travel, communications satellites and videotape had multiplied its sources to the point where even its new half-hour news show was nowhere near long enough to accommodate all the pictures it had.

Both in newspapers and television, this imposed burdens on the sub-editorial class of journalist which it was not always equipped to bear. Sub-editors are not the least literate of journalists. Graham Greene was for a while a sub-editor on *The Times* until he left to put up his plate as a novelist: of the sub-editors who (at the time of writing) help the *Sunday Times* on Saturdays, one is a Canadian scholar who edits sixteenth-century jokebooks, one is a Treasury civil servant, and three are BBC men anxious not to forget the written word altogether. But not all organisations are as well served. Sub-editors have an indispensable function: to choose sometimes from among items, and regularly from within them; and then to write words for a newscaster, or to prepare them for the printed page. Only a few of them command specialist knowledge. The conquest of time sees to it that they are supplied with a dozen political speeches every Saturday, and the pressure of time sees to it that they occasionally leave out the important parts.

Any period of time must also have a beginning. An item broadcast at the beginning of a news bulletin stands out, whether it deserves to or not; and the news organisation may then seem to be emphasising the trivial or the violent when in fact there is nothing else to emphasise.

Space is similarly unbiddable. Newspapermen sometimes wish that they could put at the top of page one, on days when no piece of news deserves special prominence, 'There is no lead story today' – just as the BBC used sometimes to announce, in the distant dinner-jacketed days of the thirties, 'There is no news tonight'. But however you arrange a pile of pages, the pile will always have a top; and however you arrange items on a page, there will always be one (or perhaps two, if you are very ingenious) which is nearer the top left-hand corner than the rest. The importance which this gives the item is not simply relative: it is absolute; and it may be unmerited.

Then again, each item has to have a headline, to say what the piece is about and to induce people to read it. In order to get as much information into the headline as possible (and to get any information at all into a heading across a single column, given the large type), the words have to be short. Short words have hard edges: they make it more difficult to blur the intent, to draw back from making an unqualified statement, than long words do. Many is the journalist who has very slightly stiffened his interpretation of his facts in order to produce a first paragraph that seems worth reading, and then been appalled to see his inference further stiffened by the sub-editor (or managing editor, or even editor) who writes the headline. Perhaps a reporter learns that an opposition politician is to visit north-eastern England to look at some of the worst centres of unemployment. He puts this together with a speech made by another opposition politician about the need for radical reconsideration of national employment policies. He says in his first paragraph that opposition leaders are actively examining a new approach. 'Labour readies new jobs plan', says the headline, in the big black letters which seem to make it not just a statement but a statement accompanied by a fist banged down. It is not exactly untrue, but it is not exactly true either. . . .

The facts of space also have their bearing on the interest displayed by all journalists in trouble, disputes, disorders. The most obvious fact about space in newspapers, or time in news bulletins, is that there is not enough of it. One reason is that a principal dread among journalists is of not being able to fill the space allotted; so they over-subscribe it instead. (Some editors believe, erroneously, that they get better work out of their staff by making them compete for publication.) Another is the sheer flow of news and newsfilm supplied by agencies – in the United States there are agencies which also supply spoken news for radio – and the volume of it offered by government departments, political parties, the embassies of foreign governments and so on. For broadcasters the pressure is especially acute: bulletins are shorter than newspapers, the broadcaster's voice delivers fewer words in a given time than the listener could have read to himself from a printed page, the impromptu speech of an interview makes its points more slowly still. So journalists, and especially broadcasters, have to make incessant choices. One rule of thumb which presents itself at once is that they should pick the abnormal rather than the normal, for the good reason that by definition there is less of it. In most societies, most of the time, order and survival and continuity are normal. At the end of any day most companies have not gone bankrupt, most aeroplanes have landed safely, most working people have stayed on the job without striking. Any newspaper or bulletin which made the normal into a news event would choke itself to death in a night. There would be nowhere near enough room. And this is a good rather than a bad sign, a sign of health. When a fish caught in the tidal Thames goes unreported, the river is presumably clean enough to make fish life normal. When a fish is news, the river is very dirty.

This is not to say baldly that the abnormal is news. Journalists do not work to definitions of news, conscious or unconscious. They know too well that the only one of any validity is tautologous: news is what you can get onto the air or into the paper. That depends in turn on such accidents as your standing in the organisation, your recent record for being right, whether you are in the office to defend your material or three thousand miles away, what else is happening, what was in the early editions or bulletins of rivals, whether details of the story were timed to break so late that room had to be reserved for it without sure foreknowledge of whether it would be interesting or not, and many more. But abnormality, divergence from present patterns, is a good start.

Simple considerations about where the facilities and the people are, again, can be highly influential. The BBC would be unlikely to lose interest in Parliament, even if the law allowed it to, while it kept a heavy investment in hardware at Westminster. Conversely, BBC coverage of India inevitably diminished in 1970 after the Corporation's correspondent in New Delhi had been expelled as a reprisal for the BBC's having shown a series of French films about India which the ORTF had already screened without mishap. In 1971, although China had joined the United Nations, there was no rush to try and set up news offices in Peking: a Reuters man was only recently free after two years' imprisonment there – again a reprisal. These are the events, quite external to journalists' own judgments, which can limit overseas coverage. Sometimes the technical considerations are less dramatic: simply that there are no satellite ground stations, no direct flights to Europe for film, the wrong internal air services, few telephones, no roads worth the name. Communicators need at any rate a modicum of communications. The main reason why there has been little coverage of the endless sporadic fighting in Chad – even by journalists from France, which once governed it – is that Chad is a very difficult place to work out of.

Henry Morton Stanley was a journalist when he found David Livingstone on the shores of Lake Tanganyika in 1871, and he had had to cope with all these obstacles and more; but (in his own account) his employer on the *New York Herald* had said to him 'Draw a thousand pounds now; and when you have gone through that, draw another thousand, and when that is spent, draw another thousand, and when you have finished that, draw another thousand, and so on; but FIND LIVINGSTONE!' Stanley was lucky. Money will open a number of doors, but it is a key which editors are reluctant to press into their reporters' hands, especially overseas. When money is tight, the foreign budget is always the first to be scrutinised with a cold eye. To the technical restraints on news coverage must also be added the economic.

In the C. P. Scott dictum 'Comment is free, facts are sacred', the *Private Eye* emendation of the last word to 'expensive' has almost as much point as the original. News organisations cost a fearful lot of money. To be able to gather and send out the news quickly calls for quantities of capital equipment – all kinds of receiving gear to get the news in; printing machinery, or studios and cutting-rooms, to prepare it; complicated transport or transmission arrangements to get it away again. All this demands capital. Now capital can be an efficient force: a chain-owned provincial paper is often better equipped than one which has kept its independence; but capital is not a radical force. People who put it up are unlikely to be enemies of the established order. They want a world where an investment keeps its value. That is a principal reason why there is a more or less marked non-radical tendency in nearly all large news organisations.

The two upheavals which have shaken the Paris offices of *L'Express*, one of the most successful news weeklies in Europe, during the past seven years have both arisen from a correct perception that success inhibits dissent. The paper made its name at the beginning of the sixties through its opposition to France's Algerian war and the methods used to fight it. In 1964 its founder, Jean-Jacques Servan-Schreiber, took advantage of its rising circulation to turn it into a magazine not unlike *Time*; and a number of his most high-minded colleagues marched off to found *Le Nouvel Observateur* as a new refuge for radicalism. Then in 1971, after briefly relinquishing control, Servan-Schreiber took it back: his published reason was that the magazine's staff had not been showing a stiff enough resistance to *'les dîners parisiens si corrupteurs'*.

So the pressure in favour of received opinions need not come from proprietors. There have been occasions when it has, true. In 1899, Edward Lloyd, the owner of the *Daily Chronicle*, shifted his paper from the Liberal to the jingo side of the argument over the Boer War: he lost most of the staff in the process, including the editor, H. W. Massingham. In the thirties the first Lord Rothermere, a younger brother of Lord Northcliffe, ran through four editors in the process of keeping the *Daily Mail* on sound pro-German lines. But these were comparatively rare instances of compulsion. Ordinarily journalists understood as well as proprietors the community of economic interest which bound them together.

The mass press has never shown any necessary reflection of the views of its mass public. The increase in the newspaper-reading public at the turn of the century, to the point where it became a majority at about the time of the First World War, was a function of the availability of cheap newspapers. It stemmed less from the 1870 Education Act than from advances in printing and publishing technology. The owner of the technology could therefore address his readers on his own terms, not theirs.

Lord Northcliffe, who (as Alfred Harmsworth) had founded the *Mail* in 1896 at a halfpenny, was the first man to make that discovery. The means by which he held his price down, advertising, is the root and ground of another large group of journalistic weaknesses. This is not because advertisers influence editorial coverage in any crude or direct sense, especially in news coverage: newspapers which carry heavy cigarette advertising have not been backward in publishing reports on the dangers of smoking. But the need for advertising has increased the tendency in news organisations to assimilate their standards to those of the money-making classes. Further, because the supply of advertising depends on the amount of spare cash which manufacturers and shopkeepers have about them, dependence on it has made news organisations dependent on movements in the economy which have nothing to do with their own success or lack of it: during the summer of 1971, when the Conservative Government waited too long before they reflated the economy and advertising was very tight in consequence, thunderous leading articles in favour of expansion were not dictated by patriotism alone. More than all that, the advertising nexus has cruelly intensified the effects of the worst scourge of journalism, which is competition. Every reader counts double: if you lose him, you lose not merely his fivepence but the element in your advertising rates which his adherence enabled you to charge. You therefore go to some lengths to keep him; and your competitors try just as hard to get him.

This competition has proved even more damaging to newspapers than their wasteful labour practices. If you are an advertiser, you decide what type of paper you want to advertise in and then go for the top paper or papers of that type. The bottom paper is starved. The two London morning papers that were forced to amalgamate in 1971 were both bottom papers. The *Sketch* ranked in point of circulation below two other tabloids, the *Mirror* and the *Sun*: the *Mail* came below another popular broadsheet, the *Express*. Exactly the same thing had happened to the *News Chronicle* when the *Mail* swallowed it in 1960. The fact that all Fleet Street newspapers are overmanned, especially among technicians, was no help; but it was not a prime cause.

It is while they are still in life, though, that competition does most damage to news organisations. It may be an antidote to the grosser forms of idleness: BBC television did at any rate throw in moving pictures with their news to match the start of a news service on Independent Television in 1955. But that negative effect is the sum of competition's virtues. When competition is for the mass audience, its natural coin is vulgarity. If Queen Guinevere wished now to maintain her assertion that we needs must love the highest when we see it, she would have to deal first with the evidence of Britain's popular Sunday press. The *Sunday People* sells nearly five million copies, and the *News of the World* over six million.

Even at the more reflective end of the market, where the competition is in terms of political rather than police-court news, the effect is almost entirely harmful. Early any evening, senior staff members can be found poring over the first editions of rival newspapers or the monitoring reports of rival news bulletins. Some accommodations are resisted, but some are made: a rejected story is brought out again, a conflicting version of another is severely questioned. It sometimes happens that two newspapers with contradictory first-edition versions of the same story, one of which must be right, will both be found to have dropped it from later editions.

This process, more than anything else, is what blurs the multiple witness which is the notional advantage of a multiplicity of voices, and gives students of news organisations an impression of homogeneity of view. If these immemorial motions are gone through for the benefit of the viewer or listener, they are pointless: he will almost certainly not see more than one television bulletin, and if he reads more than one newspaper he is most unlikely to notice discrepancies in news coverage. If they are gone through out of professional pride, they are a poor way of showing it. The only tenable explanation is that they represent, at each level, a concern for the good opinion of the man next above.

This is where the economic effects of competition multiply its journalistic effects. Historically, proprietors of newspapers (and later of television chains) lived in an atmosphere of high risk as well as high reward. They saw to it that their employees did too. The quick-hire, quick-fire methods of Fleet Street during the great circulation battles of the 1930s have been a good deal softened now; but they remain a powerful folk memory; and editors lose their jobs just often enough to keep the memory green.

The effect of this is felt throughout a news organisation, but particularly on specialist reporters, who have a defined field to cover. 'We didn't have that story': 'They had a better angle on it': a more or less unreasonable fear of losing his job, silently transmitted from the top, teaches him to forestall those observations if he can. He will therefore yield sometimes to temptation and put forward conjecture as truth, offer his own prediction as someone else's firm intention, ascribe to an eminent person an action taken at some lower level, embellish anecdote, and omit boring but necessary recapitulation in favour of unimportant but intriguing detail; and all because he knows, or thinks he knows, that his fellow on a rival paper will.

Of the eight major London morning papers, the one most consistently well spoken of by professional people outside journalism is the *Financial Times*. They are not tempted to hail it as a great cry of the human spirit, a daily summons to voyage through strange seas of thought; but they do find that it is less often wrong than its contemporaries. It cannot be altogether an accident that the *Financial Times* is the only one of the eight with a body of readers for whose attention it has in effect no competition.

CHAPTER 9

Political Imperatives

Besides technical and economic reasons, there are also political reasons which go some way to explain the evident imperfections of the way the news gets out.

If journalists do indeed live in the pockets of people in power, to the neglect of people who are not in power and not likely to be, it argues a certain brutal insight into what life is like and what their clients want. The private citizen, just as much as the citizen engaged in government, wants to learn first about people and bodies whose doings can affect him – by raising or lowering his taxes, improving or worsening his surroundings, and so on. In people with better ideas who are out of power his interest may be lively, but it will be secondary; and the more distant they are from power, the more distant will be his interest. When journalists neglect dissent, even expert dissent, and over-cultivate the established order, they are only interpreting the prime needs of the customer by sticking close to where the power is.

There is a more mechanical reason still. Perhaps in order to feel that they control at least scraps of it, people like reading about the future. A good deal of journalism is an attempt to meet this wish. A good deal of journalism, too, itself depends on fore-knowledge. You cannot turn up to report the key meeting, still less get a picture of it, unless you know when and where it is going to be held. There must be times and places written in the newsdesk diary. By far the most prolific source of them is the orderly and resourceful world of government. Governments set time-tables: oppositions only react to them. Journalists who want to witness the present and foretell the future must pay their main court to the people in power.

Or take the personalisation of political news. For television, and even for radio, this is almost a technical necessity: it is very hard to report an idea except in terms of a spokesman for it. But for all types of news organisation it is a political obligation too, at any rate in Britain. Ministerial responsibility is the name of the doctrine. The useful constitutional fiction is that the minister, the politician at the top, himself takes every decision which comes out of his department – even one like the Department of the Environment, which puts out dozens of detailed planning decisions every day, and could only get through the work on a system whereby some are not even seen by junior ministers. The minister no longer resigns if his department is shown to have made a deplorable decision, but the discovery will do his career no good; and the system is at any rate non-fictional to the extent that he must answer for the decision in public. So journalists have a good deal of excuse for seeing the measure in terms of the man. And if they try not to, the departmental press officer will try to see that they do. It will make the minister available to the press, or at any rate a statement in his name; but it will shield his officials, except from the most gentlemanly and no-names-named enquiry, with a maternal protectiveness.

This is chiefly why Whitehall is so badly reported. Constitutional theory, and civil servants' reading of it in practice, make it difficult for the journalist to get at anyone in a Whitehall department between the minister at the top and the press office at the bottom. Shortage of expertise is a cause too: journalists are often not well enough informed even to know where the gaps in their own knowledge are.

The system has virtues. It preserves a non-political civil service, and one which can speak as it finds. Officials who were publicly identified with a certain line of policy might not be wholly trusted under new masters, and with that possibility in mind they might speak less freely to their present masters. Most of them like the arrangement. They are not sorry to be spared standing up for their policies in Parliament. It is not exactly power without responsibility: a civil servant identified with a bad decision is as much haunted by it later as a minister. 'A really bad mistake is known all around Whitehall', Anthony Crosland said of civil servants after he had left office as a Labour minister in June 1970. 'The gossip that goes on is something absolutely out of this world.'

Whitehall men must occasionally sigh for the system pertaining in Washington, where officials who find the prevailing current of opinion running against them can take their case to the press. But if they invoke the aid of the press when they want it, they cannot complain at getting it when they would rather do without it. The minister would learn to look to the press as a regular party to the argument; and the officials would lose what is most precious to them, the prize for which they count wordly notoriety well lost – the monopoly of the ministerial ear. A press ignorant of the detailed arguments cannot dispute it with them.

Often it is right that the press, and therefore the public, should be ignorant of the detailed arguments going forward. For six days, in October 1962, President Kennedy kept secret the knowledge that there were Russian missiles on Cuba. It gave him time for cool discussion with his advisers: telling journalists would have meant bringing the Russians into the debate before counter-measures were decided. Commercial and economic decisions sometimes have to be taken in almost the same strategic secrecy. But a fine line separates what it is in the embattled state's interest to conceal and what it is in the embarrassed official's interest to conceal.

Britain's first Official Secrets Act became law in 1889 after a temporary clerk in the Foreign Office had covered his superiors with confusion eleven years before when he learnt by heart, and sold to a London evening paper, the eleven clauses of the Anglo-Russian treaty negotiated at the 1878 Congress of Berlin. (The pace at which stable doors were shut was slower in those days.) Stiffer acts were passed in 1911 and 1920, both remaining on the statute book; but in February 1971 the Home Secretary set up a committee of enquiry into the working of part of the 1911 act after the failure of a prosecution under it. The occasion had been the publication in the *Sunday Telegraph* in January 1970 of a British diplomat's private report on the Nigerian civil war.

The acts had not been originally aimed at the press, though the point that the press were prime traffickers in official information – missed in the charged heat of the 1911 summer – was raised in both Houses before the 1920 bill went through. But in 1932 an elderly clerk at Somerset House was imprisoned under the 1911 act for disclosing, and a *Daily Mail* reporter for receiving, details of three wills; and there were a handful of other such instances between then and the *Sunday Telegraph* case.

Officials, and even ministers, found the acts particularly useful to scare gullible reporters away with; and they had another instrument in D (for Defence) notices, warnings to editors that certain items might contravene the acts. It was a system of selective censorship set up after the passing of the 1911 act: Harold Wilson conceded, in his record of his years as prime minister, that his own attempt to call the arrangement in aid in February 1967 was one of his costliest mistakes. On that occasion the *Daily Express* had published an account of a banal arrangement for the government scrutiny of international cables which had been unchanged for over forty years. Mr. Wilson – 'gratuitously', to use his own word – complained in the House of Commons that the story was a breach of two D notices, and inaccurate as well. A privy councillors' committee found that it was neither. Mr. Wilson rejected their report. Journalists in other organisations, at least one of them in the light of direct experience, read the affair as a sign that they were increasingly expected to be in the Wilson corner or nowhere. He himself wrote: 'I was wrong to make an issue of it in the first instance. It was a very long time before my relations with the press were repaired.'

There are times when the nation's safety demands secrecy. Wartime is commonly conceded to be one of them. Yet even in time of war, once the argument has shifted from national safety to the shakier ground of national morale, concealing facts known to government can be a way of stifling discussion about whether the war in progress ought to be fought at all. It was the method used over Vietnam. When in June 1971 the *New York Times* and then the *Washington Post* began to publish copies they had obtained of the secret report prepared in the Pentagon on the origins of the Vietnam war – a publication challenged by the United States Government and upheld by the Supreme Court – admirers of the system of open government in Washington were cast down by what they learnt. The system was not as open as all that. It was not open enough to have kept the Administration from totally hiding the truth – that the main pretext for American military involvement, the 'unprovoked' North Vietnamese attack on two American destroyers, in fact came at a time when South Vietnamese guerrillas were bombarding and harassing the North under strict American control; or that the American war aim, contrary to everything said by public men, was to rescue American prestige much more than Vietnamese

democracy. As a result the informed public debate that ought
to have been a forerunner of any military action was never held.
Without the *New York Times* it would not have been conducted
even in retrospect.

The United States authorities could claim that they were not,
in the words of the First Amendment to the Constitution,
'abridging the freedom of speech, or of the press'. There are
cruder ways of doing that. In the course of 1971, to take examples
almost at random, the Pakistan army compelled Pakistani TV
to make and show films of the 'return to normalcy' in the area
of East Bengal which the army had overrun before the war
with India: the Prime Minister of Singapore forced the closure
of two newspapers and imprisoned four senior men on a third:
in Russia (where some 1500 journalists had lost their jobs in
1970, according to the International Press Institute, as part of a
political purge), people heard nothing of Nikita Khrushchev's
death for 36 hours after it happened, and then only as the eleventh
item in a radio news bulletin: in South Africa, official newspapers
themselves demanded sanctions – and looked like getting them –
against papers that dared to criticise the working of the Terrorism
Act, which allows detention without trial: in Greece, the editor
of an English-language paper was given a fine and a prison sentence for a misleading headline about Vice-President Agnew's
visit (it read 'Bombs, recruited schoolchildren greet Agnew',
which was true, but the substantiating paragraph had fallen out
by mistake): in Spain the Ministry of Information closed down
the country's only independent-minded daily paper.

And it should not be supposed that this kind of attitude
towards journalists is confined to countries with notoriously
illiberal régimes. It is not unknown nearer home; and it goes
some way to suggest another reason besides capitalist caution
why news organisations sometimes slip into a self-protective
identity of view with the powers that be. Even for journalists
in the Western democracies, keeping government sweet has a
long history. In England and America the first cautious champions of liberty were not at all sure that it ought to be extended
to journalists. Cromwell's parliamentarians believed in censorship. The first American newspaper, published in Boston in
1690, was suppressed by the Governor of Massachusetts after

one issue; and its successors showed the circumspection natural to journals published from government post offices. At the end of the eighteenth and in the early nineteenth century in England, papers which supported the Government could expect heavy official advertising and even subsidy; a succession of radical working-class papers, on the other hand, was harassed into the ground. The last of the newspaper taxes was removed in 1855; but the notion that the newspaperman should know his place in relation to his rulers persisted in the British breast. Axel Caesar Springer, the West German newspaper emperor, got his start after the Second World War by showing a proper regard for the sensitivities of the occupying British.

Some of the countries where the songs of freedom are most fervently sung have been most forward, since then, in abridging the freedom of the press. The Parliament of Ireland, in September 1971, legislated against the encouragement of certain kinds of manifestation although the new law effectively prohibited reporting them as well. The Prime Minister of France, the same month, held down the news-stand price of daily papers in the full knowledge that it would mean the death of some of the weaker – and, as it happened, the less complaisant – among them. (The arithmetic was inexorable. Average net revenue from the sale of each copy, 25 centimes: average production cost, 65 centimes: average advertising revenue, 31 centimes: shortfall on every copy, 9 centimes. Only rich papers could sit it out till their rivals fell into their laps.)

Radio and television have provided new areas for influence. In France, the brief reprise of revolutionary fervour in May 1968 did little for the Office de Radiodiffusion Télévision Française: post-Gaullist politicians continued both to hold it in line and to denounce it for suspected deviation. In the United States, President Nixon said nothing to disavow a Vice-President who called American broadcast news reporting 'a cacophony of seditious drivel'.

Broadcasting is always more open to straightforward state pressure because the state, in order to avoid literal cacophony, has to control the use of the air waves. The state also collects the revenues of state broadcasting chains, through licence fees, and regulates the take-home profits of commercial chains, through taxation. For the first fourteen months of its life, in

1927 and 1928, the BBC was forbidden to broadcast 'speeches or lectures containing statements on topics of political, religious or industrial controversy'. (The *Morning Post*, opposing the lifting of the ban, opined: 'The average man or woman, when at leisure with the world, has not the slightest desire to be plunged into disputes on any of these subjects.') During the Second World War, the Government had far less difficulty in imposing its absolute will on the BBC than on the *Daily Mirror*.

'It ill behoves those who live by the sword', wrote the *Guardian* in June 1971 during the latest bout of the Labour party's long quarrel with the BBC, 'to bleat when they cut themselves shaving.' Labour had lived by the sword: its quarrel, born out of pique at not being treated with due deference when the party was first back in office in 1964, was conducted in terms of private threats to individual staff members and public humiliation of the Corporation as a whole (notably by imposing a chairman brought across from its despised rival, the Independent Television Authority); and when BBC producers or reporters showed signs of returning a little of this animus, Labour bleated stridently. Well before the 1970 election the Conservatives began to bleat too, in case there was party advantage in it. One of the two would form the next government, and it was hard for BBC men to be sure which. ITV journalists, aware that their own comparative immunity from criticism could be destroyed by a single moment of bad judgment, watched the whole scene uneasily. Small wonder that both organisations succumbed without a blow to most of the demands which both parties made of them at the time of the 1970 election itself.

The reason why this recurrent struggle between politician and broadcaster is not fought on equal terms is that the politician has an ultimate deterrent and the broadcaster has not. Governments which license broadcasting organisations can also close them down. It is true that the BBC, being a great deal larger, would in practical terms be more difficult to replace than any constituent part of the fragmented ITV; and this might be held to explain the BBC's greater daring. On the other hand, commercial prudence might have something to do with ITV's greater docility. Working journalists, in any case, would prefer not to irritate their own superiors by obliging them even to contemplate that kind of threat.

Along with the threat comes the blandishment. The alternation of cuffs and kindnesses is a traditional technique of interrogation: politicians might sometimes be thought to have forgotten, in their dealings with journalists, who is getting information out of whom. But they find blandishment productive, in their dealings with writing as well as broadcasting journalists; and the organisation of both Whitehall and Fleet Street sometimes makes it hard to resist.

The clasp sometimes known as the establishment embrace is easily enough shrugged off. It gives, in any event, diminishing returns; even the most impressionable new editor realises in time that the information to be had at the dinner-tables of the great, to say nothing of the food, seldom repays the time spent taking it in. But there is a group of journalists, and not the least important, who live their whole professional lives within the arms of that embrace. They are the Lobby: the corps of political correspondents at Westminster.

All specialist correspondents are to some extent smothered by their sources. Many of them – specialists in defence, or the environment, or education, or the welfare services – get by far the largest part of their information from a single department of state. They are therefore very well aware that if they gave offence to that department, their work would become very difficult. They are susceptible to official suggestions that in the general interest a certain piece of information would be better unpublished. The more useful an acquaintance within the department, the less they will be inclined to use what he tells them, in order that he shall feel free to tell them more. But they are at any rate not generalists: they concentrate their knowledge on a given field; and they therefore have certain sieves through which to pass the official information they are fed.

Lobby men are specialists who are also generalists. They are the top generalists in the trade. Politics covers the whole of human life, and they cover politics. All reports made to the Government, all legislation promulgated by the Government, all parliamentarians and their rise and fall and their private causes, all Whitehall, all party activity – they have a big bag to rummage in. And they seldom have time to travel more than two hundred yards from New Palace Yard.

They are probably the hardest-working journalists in Fleet

Street. On the rare occasions when they have nothing else to do, they stand about in the members' lobby which gives them their name – the stone-flagged ante-room to the Commons chamber, where MPs pause to collect documents and messages, and to gossip. Sometimes the lobby men have no-one to talk to except each other and the policemen: sometimes the place is like a cock-tail party without the liquor, with people's eyes flickering over each other's shoulders to see who else is there. The lobby men may learn here of an early-day motion by one group of back-benchers, or an approach to the Chief Whip by another; but the real stuff of their work is not here. Increasingly, they get the word from Downing Street.

Every morning at a fixed time, and sometimes every afternoon too, they wander across Whitehall to the Prime Minister's house; and before the first hand falls on the knocker the door opens, and the doorman bows them in, and they file into the Press Secretary's rounded office overlooking the street. He tells them the Prime Minister's engagements, and then there is a half-hour exchange of loaded badinage. On afternoons when the House is sitting, to save them the walk, the Press Secretary comes across to a little turret room in the Palace of Westminster, high above the river, with the names of past chairmen of the Lobby inscribed on the wall; and on Thursdays he brings the Leader of the House with him, and sometimes the Prime Minister; and later on the Leader of the Opposition clambers up; so the Thursday night news bulletins, and the Friday morning papers, are full of strangely concordant speculation about the Government's legislative plans and the Opposition's schemes for opposing it. It may be no more than the mechanics of political life, but lobby men have a delight-ful sense of being in on the marrow of it.

At the White House, the Press Secretary talks on the record. The ethos of Washington political journalism prefers a named source. In London he talks off the record; and so does anyone else who talks to the Lobby. This privacy is so well observed that a surprising number of MPs and even ministers – to say nothing of newsdesks – are unaware of the orderly daily schedule, or the Thursday galas, or even the little turret room. That is how lobby men like it, and what their solemn etiquette demands. Besides the incidental gratifications it offers, the whole arrangement has its usefulnesses too. Except by express agreement, a lobby journalist never names his sources. This leaves him free to protect them – if he is reporting backbench mutterings against ministers, for example. It also leaves him free to invent them. It enables him, after a conversation with one parliamentary secretary, to write: 'Ministers were saying last night . . .' It even enables him to write the same thing after a conversation with one departmental press officer – whose ministers doubtless would have been saying the same thing if they could have been fallen in with. On a big day, certain evening-paper lobby men file their first stories from home before breakfast. In their account of what MPs are discussing at Westminster there is bound to be an element of conjecture.

Far more, though, the arrangement has its usefulness for the Prime Minister, his officials, the Leader of the House, and such other of his ministers as meet the Lobby when they have proposals to explain. If what they said was to be ascribed to them, between quotation marks, they would have to make sure that it was defensible line by line and did them credit. Since it is ascribed merely to 'the quarters that matter' or 'those in the know' or simply 'senior ministers', they can cast what they like upon the waters: innuendo, denigration, childlike optimism, Lear-like undertakings to do terrible things: if it floats they can derive the advantage, and if it sinks with a nasty gurgle they can disclaim all responsibility.

Lobby men would not have it otherwise. If the machinery were public, their job would look too easy. In November 1971 James Callaghan, as shadow Home Secretary, met the Lobby to talk about Northern Ireland: it is a facility open to senior opposition figures. The Conservative Government's policy was foundering, and he uttered imprecise sounds about radical rethinking. Some lobby men thought he meant really radical: the *Mail* man, in particular, had a story next morning to the effect that Mr. Callaghan would soon be suggesting direct rule and the withdrawal of all British troops. It was the paper's lead story: the headline hardened it, as headlines will, to 'Labour Pulls Out on Ulster'. To purge the resulting puzzlement, Mr. Callaghan confessed to a Parliamentary Labour Party meeting that the confusion had arisen at a lobby briefing. Lobby men were cross: if secrecy bound them, they said, it bound Mr. Callaghan too. What they also partly meant was that they disliked their newsdesks getting the idea that lobby men, so far from engaging in high-level political detective work, simply went to inefficiently conducted press conferences.

For lobby journalists, albeit among the senior reporters on their papers and with long-service stripes stretching back to Ramsay MacDonald, are by no means immune from the ordinary curses of competition. They know the terms of that competition, the anxious scrutiny by their superiors of the rival product; and they are no strangers to the slight heart-sickness of the man who fears he is losing his employer's favour, however few rational grounds he may have for apprehension. The Lobby is a large body now, with representatives from all the London morning and evening and Sunday papers, and from ITN and the BBC, and several provincial papers and groups; and it is much more active in pursuit of hard news than it was even in the early sixties, when reflections on the passing show would still do. A lobby man's principal anxiety is that he should not be scooped or left by his competitors. He will construct conspiratorial cartels in order to lessen that risk. Until not so very long ago, lobby men from a handful of Sunday newspapers, not being able to meet at the shuttered House of Commons on a Saturday, would phone each other at their offices instead to establish that none of the group was likely to put the rest at a disadvantage by knowing too much; and if a stranger answered, they would use false names.

This was harmless enough. It probably contributed to the greater good by raising the general level of knowledge. But competition also takes more pernicious forms. Lobby men will pass on forecasts of unattainable government successes ('Ministers will act soon to curb rent sharks'): they will write a story which they know to be a waste of their readers' or listeners' time, or which they suspect that Downing Street is particularly anxious for them to write in spite of its slender link with truth; and they will write it only because they know that their competitors will write it, and rather than offer long explanations to the newsdesk when the phone rings at home at midnight, they find it easier to write the story now.

The besetting sin of the Lobby, committed nightly for the same reason – that their competitors will commit it too – is to present guesswork as fact. When I was first in the Lobby I was amazed by the omniscience of my colleagues, and despaired of ever attaining it; but then I began to notice that they were in the same places as me all day, and seemed to have few special sources of information; and the seditious thought began to dawn that these confident assertions, these detailed readings of the minds of ministers, could not strictly be classed as more than inferences: inferences based on experience and evidence, but still not quite what they seemed. And these men and women (there is a handful of women among them) are a corps d'élite among journalists; and if the rest of the trade too supposes that the sun rises out of the Thames below the Terrace and sets in Parliament Square, and that pressures towards conjectural reporting need not be resisted, then the Lobby must bear its share of the blame.

CHAPTER 10

Notional Remedies

The newsboys of Amsterdam, one Saturday afternoon in May 1971, found themselves joined on the streets by journalists selling a newspaper with an almost blank front page. The workers had taken over. It was the sober, Catholic evening paper *De Tijd* that they were selling; and the front page simply said 'We'll keep *Tijd* going', and appealed for subscribers.

This particular effort at staff participation in management was brought on by the threat of the paper's closure. They did keep it going: it was still going at the end of 1971. But it was a sign of the times. There is no lack of ideas for putting the short-comings of journalism right – some of them addressed to the economics of journalism, and some to the politics; and among advocates of economic remedies, the loudest voices at the beginning of the seventies belonged to the partisans of worker control.

Of the sketches for such a system in operation, a number arose out of similar moments of alarm. In 1968 the staff of *Stern*, an illustrated news weekly published in Hamburg, went on to win a measure of self-government after their threat of wholesale resignation had beaten off a takeover attempt by an owner of more determinedly vulgar magazines. The oldest and probably the most effective of these arrangements came about in 1951 when journalists on *Le Monde* intervened to stop the paper's founder and editor, Hubert Beuve-Méry, leaving as a result of a quarrel with the board. The resulting redistribution of stock was altered again in 1968, after long negotiations, to give the staff of the paper 49 per cent of the share capital (40 per cent to the editorial staff, and the rest split between executives and clerical staff), the original shareholders (mostly Ministry of Information nominees from 1944 in origin) 40 per cent, and the management a deciding 11 per cent. By 1969 this pattern had been copied by more than thirty papers in Paris and the provinces, among them

Le Figaro – though ultimate control there remained in dispute. The idea spread to other countries. It was also developing in London. By the end of 1970 *The Times*, a little surprisingly, led the way with no fewer than three consultative committees where the management met the staff (though none of them discussed the paper's policy as expressed in leaders).

Schemes which would take a news organisation's workers past this kind of participation to something approaching control have a number of weaknesses. Workers' control seldom means *workers'* control. No one from IG Druck-Papier, the main West German printing union, sits on the editorial council of *Stern*. There are no shares in *Le Monde* for the men who unload its newsprint or mind its machines. It might be argued that manual workers are not interested. Proportionately they are probably at least as interested as journalists. Great numbers of journalists became journalists in order to write. They are glad to be allowed to get on with it. They see their editors borne down by pre-occupations which are only half relevant to journalism – buildings, wages, budgets, advertising, promotion (which means advertising the paper) – and they are grateful to have all that taken off their hands. Most journalists only become interested in the management of their paper when it has been managed with such evident ill success that it is already at crisis point.

More awkward still, a change in control does nothing to change the economic data. Newsprint still has to be bought, wage demands met, advertisements garnered, readers kept or won. Public ownership, a favourite radical suggestion, would make no difference either: not even public ownership of all organisations within a given medium, which might at least be thought to do away with the evils of competition. When those conditions were met in British television before 1955, and the BBC had a monopoly, the Corporation still felt impelled to make its audience as big as it could, in order the better to protect and finance its monopoly. Public ownership, too, however organised, can lead – as it has sometimes with the BBC – to a dangerous degree of government influence.

If public ownership is accompanied by public subsidy, either directly or through expedients like tax or newsprint-duty concessions, that danger is increased. The same is true of an idea increasingly mooted in Britain and France, a national press or information foundation. At common sites it would lease the necessary technical apparatus – printing machinery, perhaps even broadcasting equipment – to whatever bodies were prepared to hire it. The huge capital cost of starting a newspaper, in particular, would thus be avoided: newspapers would appear and disappear in some accord with what the wishes of readers dictated, and some of the capitalist pressures towards journalistic quietism would lessen. But there would need to be control over access to the equipment, if only for the sake of orderliness; and that control would in the end be exercised by the Government. It would be the problem of broadcasters and their access to the air waves all over again.

Either of those two expedients – subsidy or a national foundation – would change the economic data, true; but at a price. There are others. The one most often put forward, as a way of reducing the economic pressures which operate against good work, is to hammer the unions. The newspaper business is like any manufacturing industry to the extent that it uses machinery to produce an object for sale. But strikes in the newspaper industry are more damaging than in almost any other manufacturing industry, because none of the lost sales can be recovered. A customer deprived of his new car by a strike may wait and buy it later: a customer robbed of Monday's newspaper by a strike will not be interested in buying Monday's as well as Tuesday's the next day. Even commercial television is not so vulnerable: its only revenue is from advertisements, and many of those lost can be run later.

Because of that, newspaper owners have been prepared to go to considerable lengths to avoid strikes; and printing unions defending their members' jobs against machinery which can do more and more men's work have been able to drive hard bargains. Being paid for doing nothing, that notional nirvana of the working man, is not an uncommon experience among newspaper employees; and some of them need not even come into the building to do it. Clearly newspapers would be able to do a better job with their existing resources if some of the real wages paid to phantom wage-earners could be laid out elsewhere. But if one newspaper won this freedom, they all would, since it is their settled principle to act together; so they would all still be in the same position relative to one another, and the same

competition would rage; and it is competition which kills newspapers (by starving them of advertisements) and debases their
standards (by obliging them to deal in trivia, guesswork and the
rest). Hammering the unions, therefore, is not enough.

A more attractive way of changing the economic data would
be to charge so much higher a news-stand price for newspapers
as to reduce drastically, or even abolish altogether, their dependence on advertising. It is an idea which newspaper owners
flirt with from time to time. If it were done, it would take
newspapers back to the era before Northcliffe fashioned the
advertising crutch – before newspapers were in the mass communication business. It will not be done, because it will never
be agreed between all newspapers: the Northcliffe revolution
is irreversible. And the newspapers who would be right to object
to the idea most strongly are the best newspapers. Because news
gathering (and even arriving at well-based opinion) is very
expensive, and demands a large staff whose members can spend
days or weeks on an enquiry without feeling under-productive,
and occasions massive travel and telephone bills, it is the newspapers at most pains to get things right which are most dependent
on advertising. The 'quality' Sunday papers in London get about
three-quarters of their income from advertisements: *Le Figaro* in
Paris gets 78 per cent. If those papers lost that help, they would
have to quadruple the price to their readers; but the readers
would then be quartered in number, or something like it, and
the price would have to go up again; and this chase after a new
equilibrium would continue until newspapers were once again
circulated to a few wealthy men and institutions – the merchants
and coffee-houses of seventeenth- and eighteenth-century London.

In broadcasting, a change to a system where the whole cost
was directly borne by the customer would be even more difficult.
Systems where the customer pays directly for the programme
he receives – pay-broadcasting, with a slot for coins in the set –
have never got beyond the experimental stage. More ordinarily,
in a non-advertising system, he pays the government for permission to use the set at all, and the government passes most of
the money on to the broadcasters. But even on state chains
financed by that method, as in France and Italy, advertisements
now appear. (The system is not as new in France as has been
thought: state radio stations carried advertisements between

1930 and 1934. Advertisements lifted them out of the era when the Bordeaux Radio Orchestra consisted of the station manager on the violin and his daughter on the piano.)

Particularly in news broadcasting, advertisements have been no necessary enemy of quality. In the United States they were virtually the only source of finance from the outset; and the news services have been the only area of American broadcasting which can make even a patchy claim to excellence. For Europe, American broadcast news coverage has been a constant source of innovation, both technical and organisational – the all-news radio station is only the most recent in a long line of ideas which have been influential in Britain; and it was understood by American far earlier than by European news broadcasters that if they were to compete on equal terms with newspapermen they must acquire comparable specialist knowledge of public affairs.

Quality in news may not be the first concern of the men who back commercial broadcasting. Most of them are chiefly set on making their fortunes. This was noticeably true of the people who campaigned for commercial television in France and commercial sound radio in Britain at the end of the sixties and the beginning of the seventies. To make money, they needed to save it where they could, and the news service looked a good place to start. Plans seriously put forward by professional broadcasting consultants for stations in Britain envisaged a 24-hour service run by four journalists: they would each have had to work a 126-hour week, without holidays, to keep it going at all. But the plans introduced by the Conservative Government in November 1971 saw national and international news coming from a common news station – not an agency – in London; and well-found local news would probably be soon identified by the stations themselves as the best means to win people away from whatever else they were listening to.

There is in fact no more need for the disappearance of the commercial principle from news broadcasting than there is prospect of it. In the sense that its availability is in the end governed by how much people are prepared to pay for it, the broadcast word is subject to the laws of supply and demand in the same way as other and not less noble works of man – publicly performed music, printed books. A commercial system for broadcasting is not in itself desirable: it is ideologically neutral;

but it does at least accurately reflect the mixture of commercial
and non-commercial motives involved.

It is the practical experience of most people who work with
their brains that they scarcely notice the financial underpinning
of their work. It has very little influence on what they actually
do. The man who pays the piper is far too busy protecting his
investment, or merging it, or diversifying it, to call the tune as
well. The important thing is that, within the given financial
framework, the work should be as honestly and lovingly done
as possible.

Clearly, journalists are no more able to say that they live by
that rule than any other group of workers. Their failures are
beyond number. The question then becomes whether you seek
to correct those failures externally and *ex post facto* or internally
and in advance.

If you choose pronouncements after the event, your obvious
instrument is a press or broadcasting council – a body of wise
men, partly or wholly drawn from the industry itself, to hear
complaints and apportion blame. The Swedish press has had a
press council – called a court of honour – since 1916, and now
has a press ombudsman as well, a judge who can impose trifling
fines. The British press has a press council. The French press
was advised by a government report in January 1971 to get one,
as *une magistrature morale sur l'information*. French journalists,
hoping to have the relation between government and press
more clearly defined, are not ill-disposed to the idea. Just as
most British journalists have at one time or another written
that things are better done in Sweden, so most French journalists
have at one time or another taken the view that things are better
done in Britain.

Where these arrangements are feared, they are feared not for
their powers – they have no significant ones, beyond obliging
publication of their findings – but because they represent inter-
vention by outsiders. They are therefore for the most part
defensively met. The sequence of events has a pattern. First
comes the rising chorus of lay complaint – the Agnew phase.
The industry rejects it. The clamour is not stilled. The industry
seeks to make its peace by setting up its own private complaints
machinery: perhaps individually, as the *Washington Post* did in

December 1970 when it appointed one of its reporters resident
critic to the rest; perhaps corporately, like the Swedish court of
honour with no laymen on it except the chairman, or the British
press council in its pre-1964, newspapermen-only phase. So far
from being stifled, complaint is only stimulated. Then at last
the outsiders are brought in: in Sweden the ombudsman, in
Britain the lay chairman and lay members of the press council.

Events in British broadcasting have been following the pattern.
At the beginning of 1971 an increasing volume of complaint
against broadcast programmes came to a head when Lord Hill,
chairman of the BBC's governors, was badly mauled at a meeting
with Conservative MPs. (Is it conceivable that one reason why
the BBC is always so much more unpopular with MPs than ITV
is that – with four radio as well as two television channels – the
Corporation has many more of the plums of patronage to dis-
pense in the form of programme appearances; and for every
happy plum-swallower there are ten malcontents?) Lord Hill
concluded that Cerberus must be fed. Governors and senior
officials of the BBC evolved a scheme whereby three men retired
from very senior public offices (Lord Chief Justice, Speaker of
the Commons and Ombudsman – Sir Edmund Compton again)
should become a private complaints tribunal within the BBC.
By an odd coincidence the Independent Television Authority
was coming to much the same conclusion at the same time,
except that its committee was more evidently made up of its
own people. But when the two bodies were unveiled in October,
they had the opposite effect from the one intended. Politicians
read them as confessions that broadcasters had lost the power
to serve as trustees of the public interest. There was renewed
agitation for a broadcasting council, a body which would stand
outside the industry and quite possibly have links with Parliament; and Christopher Chataway, the Minister of Posts and
Telecommunications, agreed that such a body would now have
to be considered when the shape of broadcasting was reviewed
within the next few years.

The idea of a link with Parliament is menacing. It would hold
over broadcasters a state yoke of a kind which British newspapermen shook off more than a hundred years ago. It would com-
promise the separation between journalists and rulers. Even
without the parliamentary link, any permanent institution

carries something of the same threat – especially in Britain, where the great and good who somehow get chosen for these jobs are so very much a stage army, with a few figures constantly coming round again, and all of them bound with gold chains to the established order. The threat is lessened if the institution can only consider specific complaints, as the Press Council can; but then it is in danger of relapsing into triviality instead. In October 1971 the Press Council upheld the complaint of a peer who was cross at having been got out of his bed in Cumberland at half-past midnight by a telephone call from a reporter on the *Sun* who wanted to know whether a government grant towards a British pavilion which the peer was organising at an exhibition in Budapest was helping to subsidise pig-sticking. Of all the charges which lie against the *Sun*, bothering peers about pig-sticking is probably the least important.

The other method is to try, by internal administrative dispositions, to check certain faults in advance. Chiefly they are the faults arising from bias. You cannot make administrative arrangements to defeat inaccuracy or frivolity; but you can to defeat bias, at any rate to the extent that you can build the conflicting sides into the organisation itself. Something of this is attempted in Holland, where broadcasting time is mainly divided (after some has been set aside for a national station) between half a dozen political or religious groups in proportion to the circulations of the half-dozen magazines which set out their programmes – a barely credible system which has nevertheless proved solider than governments which tried to change it. A comparable arrangement was intended in Sweden, when a 1963 royal commission recommended that newspapers more or less closely linked to political parties should be paid a Treasury subsidy in proportion to the average number of votes which the party had won at the two most recent general elections.

Reforms seldom work as they are meant. The Swedish Parliament preferred that the subsidy should go direct to the parties – and only to parties which got their candidates elected, at that; and in consequence not much of the money went to newspapers, and none to papers outside the recognised stockade. This result was a caricature of the defect in all such systems, which is that the only oppositions welcomed into the citadel by these methods are the ones which are prepared to wipe their feet and hang their hat on the peg provided – constitutionalists whose most rooted quarrel with the present structure of power is that they are not part of it. And this is inevitable. Create institutions to express dissent and you institutionalise it: fresh dissent springs up beyond.

Dissent, again, can only be expressed in relation to a given issue. Some of those issues are permanently with us – what proportion of the national income to spend on housing or overseas aid; but some have not yet appeared – whether to fight a particular war, whether to encourage a given line of biological research. The people who differ from the received view on these issues will not always be the same people: no automatic arrangements can see to it that their voice is heard.

If political argument is to be conducted with the breath of reason rather than with the weapons of war, it is clearly vital that news organisations should find time and space for dissent. What they do passively, in phone-in programmes and letters pages, is too limited and haphazard to be useful. What they do more actively, in interviews and reviews and news reports as well as by commissioning articles, is of much greater value; and there needs to be more of it. In the end it is the news organisations which must do the choosing. The work of winnowing the fresh ideas from the stale, and the important from the unimportant, is best done by journalists; not because they are well qualified to do it, but because anyone else is worse qualified or positively suspect. This places on journalists, corporately, the burden of understanding the main developments which are at any time at issue, not just in politics, but in the many branches of action and thought which supply the political argument, from agriculture to Zen Buddhism.

It is a burden they are daily found unable to bear. But they could become better able, if they worked at it, and were encouraged. The technical imperatives are hard to answer back: many journalistic shortcomings will abide. The best chance of answering the political imperatives lies in the improvement of journalists' own capacity to see that a reasoned argument is conducted in their programmes and their columns, if nowhere else.

CHAPTER 11

Words into Action

People who run commercial television have for years been able to live by the proposition that what you see on the small screen has no effect on any of your habits except your buying habits. Violent programmes will not make you commit murder, nor libidinous programmes rape; but advertisements will make you buy.

The fact that it has been possible not merely to get away with this simple logical contradiction, but actually to make fortunes out of it, is a measure of the inspissated doubt which cloaks the whole question of the effect of mass communication on the millions who take it in.

In politics the uncertainty is particularly deep. Great sums have been spent on seeking to measure the effect of the printed or the broadcast word, and the answer remains elusive. The only real measure of political effort is electoral; yet because voters can choose what they want to hear and pay attention to, and because it is almost impossible to isolate one set of influences on them from another (present from past, television from newspapers), there is no telling what particular impulses from the world of communication went into a given electoral result.

Politicians themselves complicate the issue by winning at least part of their reputation on other battlefields. Take President Nixon and television. It is too simple a view of Mr. Nixon's career to say that he was brought back from the dead by the Checkers speech on television in 1952, worsted by the Kennedy debates on television in 1960, and rescued from the advancing Humphrey legions by adroit advertisements on television in 1968. He had after all also been congressman, senator, vice-president, Wall Street lawyer, and chief mediator to the Republican Party over the same period. The viewers had that too to judge him by. His 1972 challengers, again, had piled up at least some of their supposed electoral assets in senate seats or city mayoralties. In Britain, since parliamentary success is the main element in the choice of party leaders, it may very well be at least one element in the process whereby the electorate chooses one of those party leaders as prime minister. We cannot know. The different elements are not to be disentangled.

Some of the empirical evidence almost suggests that mass communication by itself, the form as far as it can be separated from the content, is a kingmaker of resistible power. The two portents of the French firmament who had done almost nothing in the public view before campaign television made them burst out into sudden blaze, Jean Lecanuet in 1965 and Alain Poher in 1969, fell to earth as suddenly as they had risen. Harold Wilson, taking advantage of the fine summer weather in the 1970 election to present the electorate with television pictures of his campaign caravan rather than with any reasoned defence of his record or outline of his plans, lost the job he felt sure of keeping. Indeed, there is a case for saying that during that campaign the means of mass communication worked unconsciously against him. By laying obsessive stress on opinion polls which turned out to be wrong, they encouraged Mr. Wilson first of all to call an election before he needed to and then to fight it languidly. In that sense the press and broadcasting worked against him when he had believed that they could be harnessed on his side.

But it is this belief, universal among public men, which is the important and undoubted fact. The uncertainty about political effects is crucial. Because there is no evidence on which to deny them, politicians are free to believe in them; and they need to believe in them, because otherwise their own professional lives would be founded on a doubt. They live by the word – spoken and written exposition and discussion of public problems. If the word were shown to be ineffective, they would be wasting their time. The thought is not to be thought. They therefore believe.

The fact that they believe then takes on a life of its own. For years, South African politicians have been afraid that bringing television into South Africa would give Africans ideas above their station (or that station to which it has pleased the Boers to call them). The belief could not be demonstrated; but the fact of it was enough. People in South Africa have had to do without the minor solace of television. Plans to introduce it in 1975 still left

South Africa a quarter of a century behind comparably developed
countries.

It is broadcasting which has mesmerised politicians in the past
fifty years. They have pounced successively on radio and television as magic megaphones ready to the hand. Few politicians
have used them well: a megaphone is a little too one-sided to be
an ideal instrument of communication. But politicians were
hardly conscious of that as a drawback. A greater difficulty
arose from their natural interest in the spread of political ideas.
Whose ideas were to be regularly broadcast? In a free country it
could not decently be the government's, except occasionally;
and yet so huge a power – since there could be no doubt that it
was huge – could not be left to broadcasters either.

The result was that, both in Britain and America, broadcasting
stations were forbidden to editorialise, to voice their own political
opinions or those of their staffs; and though the ukase was later
lifted in the United States, broadcasters had by then digested
the need for caution, and they treated their new freedom warily.
In Britain the ban persists. The chief means for the mass dissemina-
tion of political ideas in Britain thus remains the opinion columns
of newspapers.

On the face of it, the attention which politicians pay to leading
articles in newspapers is disproportionate at least. What is a
leader-writer beyond an anonymous spokesman for his editor
and a few colleagues? How many editors have had the political
tenacity to graduate to the status of backbencher? How many
votes has the most active newspaper proprietor been able to
command in a parliamentary division? But a number of politicians do not see it quite like that. If their words are winged, so
may other people's be. They believe in the power of verbal
persuasion to the point where they confound, in their minds,
the paper and its habitual readers. They see the words in the leader
column as being in some way transubstantiated into the opinions
of the people who read it.

It is an illusion. A good many readers left the *Observer* after,
and apparently because of, the paper's editorial opposition to the
Anglo-French invasion of Suez in November 1956. There was
no necessary identity of view between paper and reader there.
Yet politicians are inclined, when they think of newspapers and
Suez, to remember another incident. In January of that year the

Daily Telegraph had published a leader headed 'A Time for Action': it was in support of an article by Donald McLachlan on the same page which voiced disappointment with the Eden style of government. 'There is a favourite gesture of the Prime Minister's', ran the article, 'which is sometimes recalled to illustrate this sense of disappointment. To emphasise a point he will clench one fist to smack the open palm of the other hand – but the smack is seldom heard. Most Conservatives, and almost certainly some of the wiser trade union leaders, are waiting to feel the smack of firm government.'

The phrase, and the penetrating little observation on which it was founded, seem to have reverberated in Sir Anthony Eden's head. He had been Prime Minister only nine months. Whether he took the two linked pieces to be a symptom of dangerous party feeling or a likely cause of it, he treated them like messages from the oracle at Delphi. They related to indecision and timidity at home; but within seven months he found a chance to answer them with action where it came most easily to him, abroad. When President Nasser nationalised the Suez Canal at the end of July, the decision to reply with force was taken within a couple of days, and never reversed. As other politicians saw it, the influence of newspaper opinion had been reaffirmed.

Sir Winston Churchill, as befitted one of the most literate politicians of the century, was a great believer in the power of editorial policy in action. He had seen it at work. He had seen, from the inside, the respect paid to the views of the *Manchester Guardian* by the two Liberal Governments before the First World War. He had seen Asquith lose the premiership to Lloyd George in 1916 after *The Times* had disclosed and criticised a scheme whereby Lloyd George was to head a War Committee, leaving Asquith looking like what he himself called 'an irresponsible spectator.' (A quarter of a century later Lloyd George told Cecil King of the *Daily Mirror*: 'The House of Commons did not get rid of Asquith: it was the newspapers that did the trick.' They may have had a little help: there is some evidence that *The Times*'s source for the War Committee story was Lloyd George.) He had seen the BBC, as a matter of policy, refuse him what he thought his right to broadcast his disagreements with his party leader, Stanley Baldwin. He had seen Neville Chamberlain accept an arrangement with Adolf Hitler at Berchtesgaden in

September 1938 – the virtual transfer to Germany of the German-speaking part of Czechoslovakia – which had been made respectable eight days before in a leader in *The Times*. He had seen the popular press almost bring his own new Government down in June 1940 because it still contained a Chamberlain rump. It is not altogether surprising that throughout the Second World War he regarded newspapers, and the BBC, with a blend of malevolence and watchfulness. In 1942 Sir Stafford Cripps, then a colleague, told Cecil King that Churchill 'was afraid of two things: (1) the Press, and (2) that someone should become a more popular broadcaster than himself.'

That second part looks a little unfair. Churchill had no need or reason to be interested in radio popularity for its own sake. The text of his broadcasts suggests that his aim, in the general interests of what was called the war effort, was to make ordinary people feel that even in discharging ordinary tasks they bore a part in extraordinary and great events. There is no knowing whether the aim was achieved; but Churchill clearly thought it worth pursuing. When at the end of 1940 he described the BBC – the phrase is recorded in the autobiography of Lord Reith, who had left the Director-Generalship in 1938 – as 'an enemy within the gates', he will have been similarly thinking of its general effect on the climate of ideas. The most popular broadcasters in the area of current events – C. E. M. Joad and his colleagues on the *Brains Trust*, J. B. Priestley in his *Postscripts* – were also the ones most likely to question the established social order. That may have been the grain of truth in Cripps's comment. But the BBC was not in the business of passing judgment on the immediate conduct of the war. The law, the Ministry of Information and the comparative scarcity of specialist military knowledge among BBC journalists saw to that. Newspapers, on the other hand, did it all the time; and Churchill, with long experience to bear him out, believed in their power to sway the war's course. He deplored it.

Uncertain about the weight of opinion which newspapers either create or represent, politicians pay heed to them partly because of a general feeling that it is convenient, as well as right, to govern by consent. Most dealings with foreign governments are a matter of consent, too; and journalists therefore become implicated

again. Almost any government is concerned that the citizens of
a country with which it has dealings should not think badly of it.
In the late thirties, the *News Chronicle* under Gerald Barry's
editorship had the distinction of being the British paper which
most annoyed the Nazis: German officials in Berlin and London
complained repeatedly. Chamberlain sympathised with the
Germans: he was anxious that the uncompromising anti-Nazism
which spilled over into the *Chronicle*'s reporting – for example
of the Kristallnacht pogrom of November 1938 – should not
be taken to be the British Government's line. On the other hand,
Anthony Eden had been concerned in April 1935 (as a minister
in the dying Ramsay MacDonald Government) that *The Times*,
'with its defeatist leaders', should not be thought to represent
His Majesty's Government. He knew that the Germans thought
it did. Again, the uncertainty helped to turn a newspaper into a
participant.

In fact *The Times*'s attitude to Hitler was evolved quite sepa-
rately from the Foreign Office's. (It was epigrammatised in a
John Masefield poem which the paper published instead of a
leader on the morning when Chamberlain – an old man of 69,
at the end of his first journey by air – met Hitler at Berchtesgaden:

> As Priam to Achilles for his Son
> So you into the night, divinely led,
> To ask that young men's bodies, not yet dead,
> Be given from the battle not begun.

The lines were heavy with the melancholy that still clung, then
and for years afterwards, round places of classical learning –
Geoffrey Dawson, the Editor, had been at Eton and Oxford –
whose pupils had gone to a muddy death at Passchendaele and
on the Somme. *The Times*'s attitude was by no means disreputable,
nor was it unshared.) Yet Dawson and his ultimate successor as
editor, Robert Barrington-Ward, were conscious of *The Times*'s
reputation in Germany as an official mouthpiece, and often stayed
their hand accordingly. They got very little return for it in
official information. A November 1938 leader in the *Manchester
Guardian* correctly identified it as 'a misfortune, not an advantage,
for a journal to become . . . too closely connected with any
particular party or Government'. Office memories may have
spoken there. C. P. Scott had experienced the same velvet

pressures from Lloyd George, as Asquith's Chancellor, in July 1911: 'If we let Government down in international controversy,' he noted after a meeting, 'it would be inferred that they had no sufficient backing in the country.'

This notion of consistent agreement between a party and a paper is to some extent fed by diplomats and journalists from the European continent, where it is more usual. In a very long leading article in September 1971 the *Sunday Times* advocated abandoning the attempt to preserve the state of Northern Ireland and exploring a number of named alternatives instead. The piece failed of any effect it might have had because a dispute in the newspaper industry stopped the presses when they had only been running for an hour. The Irish edition got away; few others did. But the London correspondent of *Le Monde* happened to be in Ireland. He saw the leader, remembered that the *Sunday Times* had supported the Conservative Party at the end of the previous general election, and construed the piece as a sign that the Conservative Government might change its Irish policy. Sadly, no such likelihood existed at the time; but it was at any rate believed to exist for a while by *Le Monde*'s readers in Paris.

This continental propensity to regard certain newspapers as authoritative, at least if the party they support is in power, makes money a particularly delicate subject for leader-writing. Money men are not famous for sophistication: if diplomats and even foreign correspondents believe that British newspapers have unchanging policy links with parties, financiers can hardly be blamed for thinking the same thing. Devaluation of the pound, the specific for the ailing British economy which most newspaper economists would have recommended if they had felt free to, was scarcely mentioned in leader columns for the three years before it finally came about in November 1967: to mention it would have been to imply that it might happen soon, and so to renew the flight from sterling and make things worse. There was nothing to be gained by openly recommending a course of action which would only work if it was put in hand secretly. But it was a pity: officials and ministers of the Wilson Government were not often enough told how unimpressed a great deal of ordinary opinion was with the reasons why they refused to devalue – the world role of sterling, the frontier on the Himalayas, and the rest of it.

Ordinarily, leader-writers are not much persuaded of their own power. If government action follows a leading article, diplomats may regard the leader as having been a *ballon d'essai* on the Government's behalf, and backbenchers may see the incident as new evidence of the power of the press. The journalist who wrote the leader will be half aware that he was pushing at a door which was already, even if only imperceptibly, ajar. Good timing, in such circumstances, can be as influential as good arguments.

Bad timing, correspondingly, can spoil a good cause. Urging it at all can sometimes spoil it. *The Times*, anxious in November 1971 that the Parliamentary Labour Party should re-elect the cultivated and European-minded figure of Roy Jenkins as its deputy leader, made its main point the claim that he was the candidate whom Conservatives would least like to see elected. It showed a shrewd understanding on the leader-writer's part of his own unpersuasiveness. Labour backbenchers, he knew, would go to some lengths to avoid following out the wishes of leader-writers on Conservative papers. But they would go to even greater lengths to dodge doing the bidding of Conservative MPs.

Mr. Jenkins was duly re-elected. Perhaps he would have been anyway. Plenty of other forces played on the little electorate of Labour MPs.

Yet the press is more than just one pressure group among many. It speaks to all pressure groups. Some of them it supplies with arguments: some of them it derives arguments from. This again gives it a certain strength, particularly in Whitehall: ministers and officials know that the arguments in the newspapers are a distillation of the ones that have to be met. Hence the 'call for papers' when a leading article comes up with what seems to be a new and well-based plea. Hence the use made of leaders in legislative argument, both in the Commons and in the privacy of a minister's office.

This puts a premium on knowledge, on the quotient of accurate fact with which a leader is supported. There is sometimes a twitch of the official mask in face of the kind of plain-man's indignation which the *Daily Mirror* specialises in; but it is a style which can be very easily overdone. What tells is cogent argument from sound facts. If that *Times* leader did get Asquith out, it was because the facts on which the leader was based were new and true.

Is this as much as to say that the journalism of fact is more influential than the journalism of opinion? A case can certainly be made. Demands for the dismissal of ministers are the common coin of leader-writing; but the most famous, the most whole-sale dismissal of ministers took place not as the result of a leader but as the result of a news story. In July 1962 Harold Macmillan, Prime Minister for five years, his Government slipping danger-ously in the by-elections, was pressed by three of his senior colleagues to make the Cabinet changes which he intended anyway. There is no knowing when he would have done it if two days later Walter Terry, the political correspondent of the *Daily Mail*, had not given a circumstantial account of 'Mac's master plan'. It was not wholly accurate, but that could hardly be helped: the plan had not been completed. It soon was, though: Mr. Macmillan publicly gave the resulting furore of press specu-lation as a reason for rushing through a series of changes in which seven Cabinet ministers – a third of the Cabinet – lost their jobs. R. A. Butler was promoted to Deputy Prime Minister and First Secretary of State: he was widely believed to have been, at one remove, the source of the *Mail* story.

Yet these things can fall the other way. One of the ministers who lost his job was Selwyn Lloyd, then Chancellor of the Exchequer. Three years earlier he had been saved from losing his previous job, as Foreign Secretary, by a newspaper report. The political correspondent of *The Times*, David Wood, had learnt from a good source that Mr. Lloyd was not long for his present post. Mr. Wood used the information for his weekly column of political interpretation, not writing it in the style of a news story. ('We may safely accept that Mr. Macmillan has lately taken Mr. Selwyn Lloyd's arm in a paternal grip, led him to one side, and spoken from the heart. . . . Mr. Macmillan has let Mr. Lloyd know that at the Foreign Office, in these troubled times, enough is enough.')

Two accidents intervened between prediction and fulfilment. Sir William Haley, the Editor, was in the news room that night: he decided that this was the most interesting piece he was offered, and he led the paper with it as it stood, transmuting it at a stroke from a hint to an assertion. And Mr. Lloyd was in Geneva, at a foreign ministers' conference on European security. *The Times*, still read abroad as the voice of government, seemed to say that he no longer had his chief's support. Foreign Office denials of the story were not enough. Next day Mr. Macmillan had to take occasion to say in the House of Commons: 'The Foreign Secretary and I hope to carry on our work together for a very long time to come.' Mr. Lloyd stayed at the Foreign Office another thirteen months.

(That phrase, 'Enough is enough', has an unlucky history. When Cecil King – Northcliffe's nephew, and Chairman of the International Publishing Corporation – used it in May 1968 to head a signed leader on the front page of the *Daily Mirror* attacking Harold Wilson's premiership, it was Mr. King who lost his job, not Mr. Wilson.)

In both Macmillan instances, a news report influenced events. But the influence was on timing, not on the substance of the decision. Mr. Lloyd still changed his job, both times. It is much more difficult to find instances where news reporting has influenced policy; whereas policy, as in the Suez case, can be influenced by the journalism of opinion. Ministers and policymakers, after all, know more about the facts on which their policies are based than they do about the opinions to which their policies will give rise. Facts which are revelations to the world at large are often wholly unsurprising to the minister responsible: all that is new, for him, is that the world now knows. This knowledge may therefore speed up a popular decision or slow down an unpopular one; but the decision, the policy, may very well have been there already. Opinion, on the other hand, can strike wholly fresh.

Successive revelations in news columns about interrogation methods in Northern Ireland will have been less of a surprise to ministers than they were to other people: it transpired from the Compton report that there was actually a government memorandum setting them out. What the newspaper reports basically called forth, therefore, was an exercise in public reassurance. The practices continued: policy did not change or develop. But a year earlier, in August 1970, a newspaper leader had contrived to inject a new thought into the consideration of Northern Ireland's political problem by pointing out that it might be necessary to suspend the Northern Ireland Parliament for a new reason: Stormont might become inoperative, through defections by Unionist members from their own Government, as a machine to pass reform legislation. Within two days the Home Secretary, Reginald Maudling, had publicly committed the new Conservative Government in London to imposing direct rule rather than have the reform legislation abandoned. It remained his firmest policy stroke for at least a year afterwards.

It would be idle to pretend that the journalism of fact and the journalism of opinion are totally separate areas. All reporting of fact involves selection: much of the selection is made in advance – where to send a reporter, what enquiry to set on foot; and this advance planning is likely to reflect editorial interests. A paper's editorial policy is not the sum of the views of the entire staff: it represents the consensus of view among a small committee, under the editor's chairmanship, which on some papers meets regularly and on some papers not at all; but it will be generally understood by the paper's reporters, and generally approved of, in the sense that if a reporter works in a politically sensitive area and finds that he strongly disagrees with his paper he will probably try to change his field of work. (Jeremy Tunstall finds that crime, fashion and motoring correspondents are right-wingers, even on left-wing papers. If so, they can probably swallow the problems of conscience involved without too much trouble.)

The two journalisms merge, too, in the kind of signed leader-page article where comment is laced with a little information. This is a particularly American institution – the political column, the new-readers-begin-here guide and situation report (though it is not unknown in Britain too). But such articles are signed with one of a small number of names which rapidly become recognisable – a small number even in the United States, because of the syndication system; and the interested reader soon identifies the name with the standpoint, and knows what he is getting. It is a lonely form of journalism, because it rests not so much on the authority of the paper as on the soundness of the writer's own information and judgment. It can be influential; but it is very clearly the view of one man, with no proxy votes in his pocket. The anonymous leader-writer may have none either, or he may have five million; and the politician, reading him, cannot tell which.

Facts are the indispensable raw material of newspapers, certainly. A newspaper with nothing but opinions in it is as gutless as a newspaper with nothing but good news in it. (Both have been tried.) But a newspaper without opinion would be a strange, flabby mutation. A reporter who comes to grips with his subject forms opinions about it – though while he is working as a reporter he tries to keep them in check. Newspapers form opinions too. They need not keep them so rigorously in check: they have opinion columns to spill them into. They are as free to fill those columns with advice as the Government is to reject it. And they address it principally to the Government direct, not because they wash their hands of their readers (to whose solace most of the rest of the paper is dedicated); not out of any rejection of the stately processes of democracy; but simply because firmly-held opinions call for action, and this is the quickest way of getting it.

Northcliffe made a fool of himself when he declared 'the independent newspaper to be one of the future forms of government'. But one of the persuasive counsellors of government it has often been, however grudgingly heard, and will be many times more.

It goes without saying that the journalists who sit down and write the leaders measure up to their task no better than other journalists do to theirs. They ought to be both polymaths and prose stylists. They are not. The last of that line died more than a hundred years ago: Thomas Babington Macaulay. Yet Macaulay remains the apprentice leader-writer's star, his envy, his despair. It is not merely that Macaulay had a memory like a row of steel filing-cabinets. It is also that there is no reader-grappling device, no beguilement of the inner ear, which Macaulay has not thought of first. The period in two balanced parts; the short sentence capping the long one; the triad of related sentences or words; the proper name for the general idea; the rhythmic clausula – they are all there, beckoning the reader to the bottom of the page. A few chapters of his *History of England* make up the longest Irish leader ever put together, and in many ways the best. It is written from an overtly Protestant viewpoint: its centrepiece is a magical account of that symbol of Protestant success, the raising of the siege of Londonderry in 1689; yet it remains as fair as is humanly possible. It ends with the sailing of the remnant of James II's Irish and Catholic army to join him in France.

'The exiles departed, to learn in foreign camps that discipline without which natural courage is of small avail, and to retrieve on distant fields of battle the honour which had been lost by a long series of defeats at home. In Ireland there was peace. The domination of the colonists was absolute. The native population was tranquil with the ghastly tranquillity of exhaustion and of despair. . . . There were indeed Irish Roman Catholics of great ability, energy and ambition: but they were to be found everywhere except in Ireland. . . . Scattered over all Europe were to be found brave Irish generals, dexterous Irish diplomatists, Irish Counts, Irish Barons, Irish Knights of Saint Lewis and Saint Leopold, of the White Eagle and of the Golden Fleece, who, if they had remained in the house of bondage, could not have been ensigns of marching regiments or freemen of petty corporations. These men, the natural chiefs of their race, having been withdrawn, what remained was utterly helpless and passive. A rising of the Irishry against the Englishry was no more to be apprehended than a rising of the women and children against the men.'

He had improved his case a little. The 'wild geese', the exiled soldiery, were not as uniformly successful as his list makes out. He was wrong, too, in the long run: the Irishry were on their feet again within a couple of generations. But those are a leader-writer's weaknesses; and a leader-writer of his class could afford one or two.

CHAPTER 12

The Liberty to Know

Not every great and literate man would make a good journalist.
It is a job you have to respect if you are to do it properly. There
have been eminent men of letters, even eminent journalists, who
have not felt that respect. Dr. Johnson declared journalists to be
'without a Wish for Truth, or Thought of Decency'. Yet it was
Dr. Johnson who cheerfully admitted that when he was parliamentary correspondent of the *Gentleman's Magazine*, between
1738 and 1743, he made the speeches up. He wrote them in a
garret in Exeter Street, off the Strand, his hand travelling faster
over the paper than most people could write from dictation:
sometimes he had no better information than a list of the speakers
and the side they took, and often he had none at all. The press
was formally barred from the Commons at the time.

That buccaneering spirit has never quite died in English journalism – the pretence that the sheer difficulty of getting any information at all justifies peddling bad information, or the assump-
tion that no one could be silly enough to believe in the total
veracity of the product. (Dr. Johnson gave the job up when he
found that his invented speeches were thought genuine, and had
the grace to be ashamed of the exercise for the rest of his life.)
I can remember finding examples of that spirit when I was first
a journalist at the end of the 1950s. To judge by results, there
are offices where it flourishes still.

The obstacles of time and place have always bulked large in
journalism; and overcoming them better than one's competitors,
and winning praise for it from one's colleagues, has always been
one of the authentic pleasures of the trade. Another great man
who passed this way, Charles Dickens, caught that peculiar
zest definitively when he looked back from a Newspaper Press
Fund dinner in 1865 to his time as a political reporter thirty
years before. 'Returning home from exciting political meetings
in the country to the waiting press in London, I do verily believe

I have been upset in almost every description of vehicle known in this country. I have been, in my time, belated on miry by-roads, towards the small hours, forty or fifty miles from London, in a wheelless carriage, with exhausted horses and drunken post-boys, and have got back in time for publication, to be received with never-forgotten compliments by the late Mr. Black, coming in the broadest of Scotch from the broadest of hearts I ever knew. These trivial things I mention as an assurance to you that I never have forgotten the fascination of that old pursuit. The pleasure that I used to feel in the rapidity and dexterity of its exercise has never faded out of my breast.'

Any reporter who has worked hard in any branch of the business would recognise the essential truth of that picture still. There is a Mr. Black in most offices. Substitute fogged airfields for miry by-roads, and ham-handed telex operators for drunken post-boys, and journalism in the 1970s offers exactly the same perverse charm. But Dickens – and here is the point – did not suppose, as Johnson did for a while, that it was enough just to finish the obstacle-course and get his copy into the office in time. It had also to be the right copy. The accuracy of his short-hand, and of his transcription of it for the printer, was as much a point of pride with him as his reliability in getting the story home. He respected his employment.

Because of that, he did a journalist's proper work. When in May 1835, for the *Morning Chronicle*, he helped report a by-election in South Devon which Lord John Russell had to fight (as was then the practice) on being appointed Home Secretary and Leader of the House, Dickens was supplying the capital with news of the developing opinions of the most important and independent-minded member of the new Melbourne administration. The *Chronicle*'s most careful reader will probably have been Melbourne himself. Dickens was in the business of government.

Most journalists are uneasy at the notion that they are in some way serving the interests of government. They would rather feel that they are working on the other side. But it is possible to be part of the process of government without being a branch of Her Majesty's Government. More than that, there is a sense in which all citizens are in government now: not just because Britain is a fairly responsive democracy; not even because, in a complicated modern state, power is infinitely diffused: but because we now know that we cooperate or perish. In the days when Dickens was a journalist, it still made sense for journalists to suppose that total liberty of individual action was both desirable and attainable, and that it was that liberty which they were defending against a predatory state. But in the late twentieth century, when all families and all nations need to surrender part of their economic sovereignty if they are to save some of their number from an offensive and dangerous degree of poverty, and when the actual survival of tolerable life is in question unless man's liberty to do what he likes with his surrounding air and land and water is substantially limited, libertarianism looks less helpful than it did. If politics, national and international, becomes – as it ought – increasingly a matter of the negotiated sacrifice of liberty, journalism has an inescapable part in it as the way for all sides to be heard.

There is also a narrower point than that. Although it may be true that the entire citizenry is engaged in politics, some of its members are more actively engaged than others. It is within the observation of all political journalists that the people who study their output most sedulously are politicians. They need it most, both to hear and be heard: they cannot work sensibly without it. If Edmund Burke did say that parliamentary press gallery reporters are a fourth estate in parliament (no vertiginous eminence: the bishops are the first estate, after all, followed by the lords temporal and the commons) this is all he can be taken to have meant. Journalists are part of the machinery.

The idea that journalists are a part of government makes a number of politicians uneasy too – particularly politicians whose sayings and doings are excluded from journalistic reports, or reported with unfavourable comment. Both exclusion and comment are a criticism. The politician denounces the critic as self-appointed. The denunciation is not wholly fair. On the point of fact, no-one appoints himself as a reporter or leader-writer or television interviewer: he is appointed by his editor, so he has undergone some process of choice. But not of election, retorts the politician. It is not a clear case. Journalists work for an organ which the reader or listener or viewer has chosen. He has chosen it from a fairly restricted field: a television news organisation from among two, perhaps the same for radio news, a tabloid newspaper from among three, and so on. But the MP with 40,000 voters at his back was presented to them as part of an equally narrow choice. Newspapers and broadcasting organisations can claim, if they get into an argument about it, to represent their clients in at least as real a sense as politicians can.

To be part of the process of government is not an aim shared by all journalists or all journalistic organisations. A man I know was hired to write a weekly political article for a very popular Sunday newspaper. No-one on the paper's senior staff offered any ideas; and in the absence of stimulus, he found his pieces getting duller and duller. Yet the editor's satisfaction, each week, increased in proportion to the tedium of the articles. So did the writer's puzzlement – until he realised that he was in fact the paper's figleaf, its only attempt to pretend to its readers that it or they were interested in anything else beside tales from the magistrates' courts; and as such the duller, the more impenetrable, the better.

The fact that such newspapers sell so well is a reminder that the species man is imperfect, and that therefore the sub-species journalist must be imperfect too, and sometimes do its work badly, like every other sub-species. Because the nature of man will not change, the nature of journalists will not change either. But journalists are not absolved by the fact of their human imperfection, any more than anyone else is, from trying to do better; or, to put the point in less doctrinal terms, there are plenty of things which journalists do wrong which they could do right if they thought about it.

They could know more. In general, over a period of years, the trade could become better educated. In detail, there is no journalist who would not profit from a better knowledge of the fields he covers. And this is not impossible to achieve. It is a matter of what is admired in news offices. If more news organisations were prepared to compete in terms of the truthfulness and well-groundedness of their exposition, and fewer in quantities of trivial fact compiled, levels of journalistic knowledge – and then of knowledge among our rulers, and perhaps in the end of public knowledge – would rise.

Journalists could use words more carefully. They are nothing like such murderers of words as are most of the people whose words they report, true. They could nevertheless see to it that when they use, or report the use of, phrases like increased prosperity to mean the faster consumption of natural resources, or development to mean devastation, or deep interrogation to mean torture, or military solution to mean military repression, they enter the necessary caveats. Such a policy would not be seen to be fair: the volume of complaints against news organisations would greatly increase; but it would be fair.

The chief responsibility for such healing pedantry would lie with newspapers, as the chief stewards of the word in public affairs. From it a number of good consequences would flow. Public men who found their public utterances so rigorously glossed might occasionally be a little more careful of what they said – a beginning in itself to the search for an antidote to the politics of unreason; and journalists who taught themselves to be scrupulous about words might in time become more scrupulous about facts.

It is here that academics should tackle journalists. Teachers and students who scrutinise the work of journalists tend to do it with a sociologist's fatalism: they take it as read that journalism is full of faults, and then they examine what it is about journalists which makes them prone to commit faults – when they left school, what they do in their spare time, how they vote. It might be worth the while of academics to borrow a technique or two from the subject of their study. If journalists become interested in a situation where work is being faultily done, they examine the faults first; and if they think the evidence of faultiness sound and important, they publish it. They may also hazard a view as to why the people concerned should have behaved as they did; but that would be hardly worth publishing, if publishable at all, without the factual evidence. The facts may well be in the past now; but the report has at least some hope of seeing to it that the same abuse is not repeated. If you show that Labour party ways of choosing candidates for Parliament are in general open to abuse, nothing much will happen. But if you show – after the event – that in a particular constituency, Islington North, before a particular by-election, in October 1969, at least two particular delegates to the Labour selection conference were impersonated by people who can have had no right to be there, then – although the result of that by-election will be unaffected – party workers at headquarters and all over the country will go to a great deal of trouble to see that all their procedures are more effectively proofed against manipulation in the future. They would prefer not to have the same finger pointed at them.

If university people who study journalists' work share journalists' natural interest in improving the situations which they observe, then they could do worse than copy this part of journalistic behaviour. They should examine specific examples of journalistic work, after the event. They should consider the way the passing of the 1971 Immigration Act, or Labour's change of line on the Common Market, or internment in Northern Ireland, were reported at the time. They will have the advantage that facts not then known will have come to light since, that policy not then disclosed has now been revealed, that forecasts then made will have been proved true or untrue. They will be able to test at leisure the accuracy, fullness and fairness of what journalists wrote and broadcast in haste. Such examination cannot threaten journalists, as long as it is not linked to the state through any kind of institutional machinery. But its findings may sometimes chasten and mortify them; and some journalists may even change some of their ways as a result. There is academic work of this kind done already, but not nearly enough.

What journalists do deserves this degree of regulatory examination. If – to sum up – they do their work well, they can be the enemies of unreason in public affairs: this responsibility is especially entrusted to newspapers, which show no sign of being deposed from their leadership by any electronic revolution. They can oppose and expose unreason as they go about their daily and weekly work of ferrying information and ideas between the various levels of government and between government and governed. They often fail of this duty, or discharge it badly. Some of these failures can be written down to the given technical and political circumstances within which they work, and some to a straightforward failure of understanding. But they have often influenced the thoughts and actions of public men – partly because most public men believe in the unproven influence of journalists on the opinions of people at large. Even in the comparatively narrow context of government, they are therefore important, and the number of their failures worth reducing. The failures that arise from technical and political restraints are hard to eliminate, though that does not absolve the trade from trying to work on the restraints and remove them. The ones that follow from a lack of understanding could be lessened in number by action and application on the part of journalists themselves; but they need the same kind of stimulus and encouragement to self-improvement from outside as they themselves supply to back-sliders in other paths of life. The best source of that stimulus – the only source from which it can come without increasing the already damaging political pressures on journalists – is the study of finished journalistic work at universities and colleges.

Journalists tend to write and speak as if the only threat to the excellence of their product came from outside it – from any of the unwelcome persuasions either to speak or to keep silent which are gathered together in the word censorship. But censorship is only part of the threat. The wider threat is of a general under-valuing of words as an instrument for reasoned discourse between people. Journalists themselves contribute to that devaluation every time they are careless in their use of words, their exposition of facts, their deployment of arguments.

'Give me the liberty to know, to utter, and to argue freely according to conscience, above all liberties.' It is one of Milton's last demands of the Long Parliament in the *Areopagitica*. 'The liberty to know' is a peculiarly well-filled phrase. The liberty, and not the right: the reader cannot demand knowledge, he can only demand the opportunity to acquire it: the labour of learning must be his own. And to know, not just to have opinions which may or may not be well based: if he wants knowledge, he must have the proper information, as full and accurate as can humanly be had.

This knowledge, further, is the preliminary. Only when it is absorbed can there be utterance and argument. The reader, perhaps, asks no more than to know: it is already a considerable demand. But the writer, the journalist, asks also to utter and to argue freely. He must first know, and offer the same opportunity to others. Without that, he has not earned the liberties that go with it.

A NOTE ON BOOKS

I venture here a list of those books which a reader pursuing these themes further might expect to find most illuminating.

The case for believing that the word is dead has been best stated by George Steiner in his moving book, *Language and Silence* (Faber & Faber, 1967; Pelican, 1969). His later set of four lectures, *In Bluebeard's Castle* (Faber & Faber, 1971), is marginally less pessimistic.

There is a great deal of interesting material on strategic broadcasting, notably General de Gaulle's from London during the Second World War, in the third volume of Asa Briggs's History of Broadcasting in the United Kingdom, *The War of Words* (Oxford, 1970).

The two most useful general books about modern newspapers are Francis Williams's *The Right to Know: the Rise of the World Press* (Longmans, 1969) – a journalist's account of the historical background to the state of the press in several countries, especially Britain and America; and Colin Seymour-Ure's *The Press, Politics and the Public* (Methuen, 1968) – an academic's account of how newspapers operate in politics. The story of one serious-minded newspaper's operations over 150 years is told by David Ayerst in *Guardian: Biography of a Newspaper* (Collins, 1971).

The most spirited statement of the charges that can be brought against the British press is in a collection of essays mostly written by journalists and edited by Richard Boston: *The Press We Deserve* (Routledge & Kegan Paul, 1970). Journalistic shortcomings in a particular context are documented in the chapters on broadcasting (by Martin Harrison) and on Fleet Street (by Colin Seymour-Ure) in *The British General Election of 1970*, by David Butler and Michael Pinto-Duschinsky (Macmillan, 1971).

The extent to which the growth of the popular press was a function of technology and commerce, rather than of any positive demand by its readers, is explained by Raymond Williams in

The Long Revolution (Chatto & Windus, 1961; Pelican, 1965).
The details of the life of the man who first perceived and used
this opportunity, Lord Northcliffe, are set out with great industry in *The House of Northcliffe*, by Paul Ferris (Weidenfeld
& Nicolson, 1971). The history of the British press is at present
written in scraps. An account of the still unfinished struggle over
the Official Secrets Acts is given in Jonathan Aitken's *Officially
Secret* (Weidenfeld & Nicolson, 1971).

Books which touch on the effects of journalism are mainly
concerned with its effects on the public at large. David Butler
and Donald Stokes, in a chapter in *Political Change in Britain:
Forces Shaping Electoral Choice* (Macmillan, 1969; Pelican, 1971),
consider newspapers at least as much as television. Most other
work sticks to television: a convenient compendium of the state
of modern knowledge there is a collection of five papers edited
by James D. Halloran, *The Effects of Television* (Panther, 1970),
including one by Jay G. Blumler on political effects. Another
paperback, by a Sorbonne sociologist, has thoughtful material
on the French presidential election of 1969: it is *Les Pouvoirs de
la Télévision*, by Jean Cazeneuve (Paris: NRF/Gallimard, 1970).
The most readable book in this field is *The Selling of the President
1968*, by Joe McGinniss (Andre Deutsch 1970; Penguin, 1970):
it is not so much a statement that Richard Nixon won the
American presidency through television commercials as a satire
on the people (including Mr. Nixon) who believed that he could.

Works which consider the impact of journalism on public
policy are much fewer. Franklin Reid Gannon compiles valuable
evidence in *The British Press and Germany 1936–1939* (Oxford,
1971); and Cecil King's Second World War diary *With Malice
Towards None* (Sidgwick & Jackson, 1970), and the Briggs third
volume mentioned earlier, are both full of examples of the crucial
element here – the belief on the part of public men that journalism influences voters, which is what produces their inter-
mittent readiness to adjust their own behaviour accordingly.

The best example of what seems to me the right kind of academic study of journalism is *Demonstrations and Communications:
A Case Study*, by James D. Halloran, Philip Elliott and Graham
Murdock (Penguin, 1970), in which three men from the Centre
for Mass Communications Research at the University of Leicester
examine the way a march through London in October 1968

in protest against the Vietnam war was reported by seven London morning papers, the BBC and Independent Television: they show that newspapermen and broadcasters, having decided in advance that the occasion would be interesting not as a demonstration of political belief but simply as a fight, played up the incidents which bore out this reading and played down the ones which did not. Plentiful examples of the alternative, head-counting, approach to the study of journalism are to be found in *Media Sociology: A Reader*, edited by Jeremy Tunstall (Constable, 1970). Mr. Tunstall's own books about journalism, both based in part on the questionnaires mentioned in Chapter 6 above, are *The Westminster Lobby Correspondents* (Routledge & Kegan Paul, 1970) and *Journalists at Work* (Constable, 1971).

INDEX

INDEX